Up the
GREAT NORTH ROAD

Up the
GREAT NORTH ROAD
The Story of an Ontario Colonization Road

JOHN MACFIE

The BOSTON
MILLS PRESS

A BOSTON MILLS PRESS BOOK

Library and Archives Canada Cataloguing in Publication
Macfie, John, 1925-
    Up the Great North Road : images and impressions of an Ontario colonization road, 1867 to 1967 / John Macfie.

Includes bibliographical references and index.
ISBN 1-55046-421-3

1. Great North Road (Parry Sound, Ont.)--History. 2. Parry Sound (Ont. : District)--History. 3. Land settlement--Ontario--Parry Sound (District)--History. 4. Millin family. 5. Macfie family. 6. Macfie, Frank Nicholson.
7. Millin, Mary Catherine. I. Title.

FC3095.P37M35 2004   971.3'15   C2004-902874-X

Publisher Cataloging-in-Publication Data (U.S.)
Macfie, John, 1925-
    Up the great north road : images and impressions of an Ontario colonization road, 1867 to 1967 / by John Macfie.
[144] p. : photos. ; cm.

Includes bibliographical references and index.
ISBN 1-55046-421-3 (pbk.)

1. Ontario--History--19th century ˆ Pictorial works. . I. Title.

971.303 dc22   F1058.M33 2004

Published in 2004 by BOSTON MILLS PRESS
132 Main Street,
Erin, Ontario N0B 1T0
Tel 519-833-2407
Fax 519-833-2195
books@bostonmillspress.com
www.bostonmillspress.com

IN CANADA: IN THE UNITED STATES:
Distributed by Firefly Books Ltd.   Distributed by Firefly Books (U.S.) Inc.
66 Leek Crescent   P.O. Box 1338, Ellicott Station
Richmond Hill, Ontario L4B 1H1   Buffalo, New York 14205

The publisher acknowledges for the financial support of our publishing program the Canada Council, the Ontario Arts Council, and the Government of Canada through the Book Publishing Industry Development Program (BPIDP).

Design: PageWave Graphics Inc.
Printed in Canada

This book is dedicated to the memory of Frank Nicholson
Macfie and Mary Catherine Millin, who separately joined the
19th-century migration of agricultural settlers up the Great North
Road and in due course became my grandparents.

Jim Canning, who was born at Caledon, Ontario, in 1870 and came with his parents to McKellar at age six, was photographed in 1959 reminiscing about the old days.

Contents

For years after tractors shouldered the burden of farming "out front" in southern Ontario, real horsepower prevailed in Parry Sound District. Here, Gordon Whitmell plows a field near Dunchurch.

Preface

————◦————

IN 1870, JAMES MACFIE, a middle-aged bachelor of Scottish birth, crossed
Georgian Bay from Collingwood, Ontario, to the fledgling village of Parry
Sound, where he found work with a crew clearing a wagon road into the hinterland.
Ten years later, my grandfather Frank Macfie followed his Uncle James up that
road, forging the second link in a chain of events that led eventually to this book.

The path these forebears of mine followed was the Great North Road (also
variously called the Great Northern Colonization Road, the Northern Road, or
simply the North Road), one of a score or more colonization routes that, beginning in the 1850s, the government pushed into the rock-ribbed southern flank of
the Precambrian Shield to admit agricultural settlers. The circumstances of my
twice-great-uncle James Macfie's coming to Parry Sound are somewhat hazy. In a
memoir composed in 1935, my grandfather speculated as to why his uncle "was
deluded enough to come out to try his luck in Canada when he had a good job [as
an inspector of fisheries off Scotland's west coast] at home," and concluded, "no
doubt there was a woman at the bottom of it." James's brother William had
preceded him to Canada, filed papers on a homestead lot near Collingwood,
Ontario, then returned home and signed over his claim to James. On reaching
Collingwood, James found someone else occupying the property, which perhaps
had been forfeited for non-performance of location duties, so he boarded a
steamer and forged on to the new frontier, Parry Sound.

Some 40 kilometres north of Parry Sound, the blazed route of the Great
North Road broke clear of a rocky and swampy stretch to enter a relatively level,
deep-soiled tract treed by maple, birch and hemlock. A strong component of
hardwoods in the forest makeup was taken as an indicator of good soil beneath,
and it was here, on Lot 49 of Concession A of the Township of Hagerman, that
James Macfie threw down his government-issue axe and shovel and staked his
homestead claim. A decade later, in August 1880, my grandfather, a 30-year-old
marine engineer newly returned to Scotland after a lengthy tour of duty with a
rice-growing concern in Burma, decided to visit his father's brother James in the
wilds of Canada. Legend has it that, after reaching Parry Sound and trudging
what he calculated to be the right distance up the Great North Road, Frank
stopped at a shanty to ask where he might find the homestead of James Macfie.
The settler replied, "See yon man cradling oats just over our line fence? That's
Jimmy Macfie." Frank walked on and waited until the harvester's round of his
field brought him to the roadside, then hailed his uncle.

Having nothing more pressing to do at the moment, Frank elected to stay on
for a few months to help his uncle enlarge his small clearing, and generally
improve upon the rude circumstances — his home was just a rough shanty and
his means of getting about was a jumper pulled by one of his cattle — in which he
found him. One day late that winter while they were chopping a fallow, the pair

undertook to fall a large yellow birch tree. The clumsy approach to this difficult task, by men hailing from the treeless west coast of Scotland, can be imagined. After carefully studying the great tree's form and stance (as Frank would recall later in life) they agreed on the direction it was naturally inclined to fall, then set about chopping into the base of the trunk, one man working from each side. But they had failed to weigh the effect of one extra large, diverging limb, and as the birch began to topple it pivoted unexpectedly on the stump, changing the course of family history by striking James in its fall and fracturing his thigh. Frank thus found himself obliged to extend his excursion in Canada while he cared for his invalid uncle and his few livestock, and the stay became permanent.

Forty-five years later, in 1925, I was born on that farm, and during my formative years the Great North Road was the road to everywhere. I still regularly drive a 50-kilometre section, now incorporated into Provincial Highway #124, that links Parry Sound and Dunchurch, so I know it as well as anyone. However, I could not have produced this book without much help. A good deal of the background information is derived from notes and tape recordings I made during half a century of interviewing descendants of the pioneers. I made considerable use of material in the Parry Sound Public Library and the West Parry Sound District Museum, and the microfilms of the *Parry Sound North Star*. I also drew on the resources of the Ontario Archives, which holds collections of Duncan F. Macdonald's letters and photographs, and on archival material held by the United Church of Canada. An old friend and retired land surveyor, Hannes Hietala, ferreted out archival records that I would never have discovered myself. A number of previously published works served as valuable sources of quotations and background information. These include: *Muskoka and Haliburton, 1615-1875* by Florence B. Murray, *Guide Book and Atlas of Muskoka and Parry Sound Districts* by W.E. Hamilton, *McKellar Memories* by Evelyn Moore, *History of Northern Parry Sound District* by Everett Kirton, *Along Memory Lane with Hagerman People* compiled by the Dunchurch Women's Institute, *God's Country* by Rev. John Firmin, *By Northern Lakes* by Rev. W.W. Walker and *Star Gazing* by Laura Knight Heidman. I am also indebted to Albert Langford for allowing me to quote from the diary of his father, Percival, and to the Whitestone Historical Society and Michael Powell for letting me use snapshots and poetry from the photograph album of Michael's father, Gordon Powell. The photographs of recent vintage are largely my own, while earlier images were borrowed from numerous private and public sources. Wherever possible I have assigned credit lines to contributed pictures. But for the generosity of the many people who agreed to share their memories and photographs, this book could not have been published. Not least, I thank my daughter, Elizabeth, for proofreading and editing the manuscript, and my wife, Joan, for her suggestions, her proofreading during production of the book, and for her infinite understanding and tolerance while I neglected normal duties in order to focus on illuminating the path of the Great North Road.

Frank, Catherine and Teddy Macfie deliver their contribution
to a wartime scrap drive to the roadside, about 1941.

Courtesy of Edith Macfie

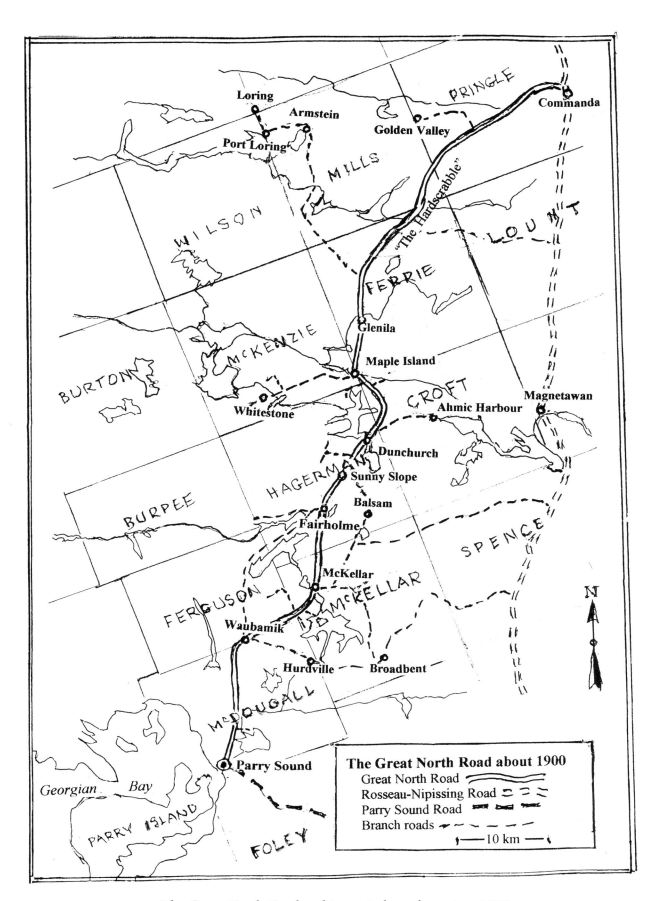

The Great North Road and its main branches, circa 1900.

CHAPTER ONE

In the Beginning

THE REGION PENETRATED by the Great North Road had long been visited seasonally by Algonquian-speaking Natives making hunting and gathering forays to the interior from their home communities along Georgian Bay. The custom still prevailed in 1870, when seven-year-old Mary Millin arrived with her homesteading parents, Arthur and Jane Millin, at the future site of Dunchurch. Following is an excerpt from a memoir Mary compiled nearly half a century later:

> There were some Indians camped at the Narrows who used to visit us often. They were Christian Indians and could speak the English very well. One of them named John Pegamagoba would come and listen to father reading Pilgrim's Progress. He took a great fancy to the book because it was illustrated with bright coloured pictures which he seemed to enjoy looking at and talking about, so my father gave it to him. Then he came one day with a lovely roast of venison for our Christmas dinner which we all enjoyed.... One time we had an Indian service; there was quite a number of them camped on the hill that is now called "the Grange Hill," and among them was a preacher [possibly Rev. Allan Salt of Parry Island, a Methodist minister]. So they came on a Sunday and had a service in our house, and the preacher spoke first in English then in Indian....

The area surrounding Whitestone Lake was then a deeryard, where deer congregated to survive winter under sheltering conifers. When a writer, quoted in *The Guide Book & Atlas of Muskoka and Parry Sound Districts*, visited Dunchurch in the winter of 1874–75, he was taken to a nearby Native hunting camp:

> Having reached the camp, a striking scene broke on view. The Indian, with that exquisite instinct which seems his heritage, had pitched his tent in such a position with reference to a very large square boulder, that the camp was completely sheltered from the wind and cold. Between the boulder and the camp was a roaring fire.... Deer-skins were hung on poles, the meat was being got ready for transport.... Next day I saw an athletic young Indian yoked to a kind of harness, and dragging a large quantity of venison wrapped up in a deer-skin, which itself (with the hair so disposed as not to catch the snow) formed the vehicle of transport.

The arable parts of southern Ontario now being fully taken up, the government, soon after the middle of the 19th century, resolved to maintain the momentum of settling Canada West by opening up the Ottawa–Huron Tract, lying between the lower Ottawa River and Georgian Bay. There, wrote the Commissioner of Crown Lands for Upper Canada in his report for 1856, "natural barriers presented by extensive rugged and comparatively barren tracts were such as to be insurmountable to individual enterprise." If the government would provide roads, it was reasoned, the natural reluctance of agrarian settlers to enter this rugged territory would be overcome.

This stone spear point, judged to be several thousand years old and unearthed on an island in Lorimer Lake, may have been used for killing caribou not long after the end of the Ice Age.

Overlooking the fact that the Precambrian Shield as potential farmland was mostly gristle and bone, land surveyors were dispatched to grid it into 100-acre homestead lots. Ottawa allocated funds, and at intervals along the southern flank of the shield, crews of labourers began hacking out colonization roads following the line of least resistance. At the same time, prospective settlers were invited to find their way in and stake location claims, a process that would be formalized in 1868, when the Ontario legislature passed its Free Grants and Homestead Act. One of the colonization roads, the Rosseau–Nipissing, commenced at Rosseau, at the head of the lake of the same name and steered due north toward Lake Nipissing. Its purpose was to bring settlers into central Parry Sound District, utilizing the navigation potential of the Muskoka Lakes as a way in from the settled south of Ontario.

Until a branch of the Northern Railway reached Lake Muskoka in 1875, the vanguard of these settlers made their way in from Lake Simcoe via the Muskoka Road, construction of which had begun 15 years earlier.

The Great North Road was meant to similarly exploit Georgian Bay and the excellent natural harbour offered by Parry Sound as a portal to western Parry Sound District. Parry Sound, the water body, was so named by the Royal Navy's Lt. Henry Wolsey Bayfield following his survey of Lake Huron in the 1820s, after Rear-Admiral Sir William Edward Parry, one of the more successful participants in England's hunt for the Northwest Passage. The site of the future town of Parry Sound, at the mouth of the Seguin River, was a seasonal gathering point for local Ojibway. Seguin evidently derives from *see-kwun,* the Algonquian word for spring-time; perhaps fishing in the rapids where the river makes its final plunge into the sound, or maple sugar-making upstream, drew people there at that time of year. European presence dates from 1856, when the Crown granted William M. and James A. Gibson of Willowdale, Ontario, 100 square miles worth of timber-cutting rights flanking the lower reaches of the Seguin River. They installed a small sawmill, drawing power from the lowermost rapids on the Seguin, and began logging pine along the banks of the river. In 1860, William Gibbard, who later wrote about his tour of Georgian Bay, visited Parry Sound and observed that the Gibson mill was shipping lumber to the distant port of Chicago. Gibbard also ventured to guess that Parry Sound was destined to become "the lake depot of a large and good back country."

In 1863, the Gibson interests were acquired by the partnership of William Beatty and his sons William and James, of Thorold, Ontario. The Beattys then consolidated their foothold in Parry Sound by purchasing from the Crown

The water-powered Parry Sound Lumber Company sawmill at the mouth of the Seguin River in May 1885. The Great North Road crosses in front of the cluster of houses on the right.

Courtesy of Parry Sound Public Library

Walter Beatty's survey crew in the Parry Sound woods in 1870. When J.W. Fitzgerald surveyed his line from Sault Ste. Marie to Parry Sound in 1865, his crew consisted, in addition to himself, of two chain-bearers, two explorers (who ranged ahead seeking the best route) and 11 axemen.

2,200 acres encompassing much of the future townsite. The younger William soon assumed control of the family's Parry Sound enterprises, enlarging lumbering operations (his sawmill employed 70 men in 1869), opening a general store, and selling village lots to incomers. Other lumbermen were attracted to the sheltered harbour, and in due course three large sawmills situated on the inner sound were exporting millions of board feet of pine lumber annually to markets up and down the Great Lakes.

A staunch Wesleyan Methodist, Victoria College-educated William Beatty preached the town's first religious sermon in the cookery of his sawmill, built its first church, and worked diligently to discourage the consumption of liquor, then widely regarded as the scourge of rural Canadian society, in his newfound community. He took an active interest in the welfare of the Natives of nearby Parry Island Reserve, prevailing upon Ottawa to help fund a day school and agricultural development on the reserve. In a bid to enlighten the "benighted Pagans" among the Native population, Beatty inaugurated open-air preaching sessions in a pine grove bordering a sandy beach on his property in Parry Sound, and as years went by the annual camp meeting at the foot of Belvedere Hill grew into an event drawing people, both Native and non-Native, from far and wide.

And unlike most lumbermen, who opposed agricultural settlement, using the argument that land clearing by settlers deprived them of trees that ought to be theirs, and that runaway fallow fires destroyed additional large quantities of timber, William Beatty promoted immigration to the district, and went to considerable lengths to build roads to admit them.

When the Beattys arrived in Parry Sound, the community consisted only of Gibson's little sawmill, a store, and half a dozen log shanties. They immediately began pressuring the government to fund an overland access route — the Parry Sound Road — to cross-connect with the Rosseau–Nipissing and Muskoka colonization roads. Within months, young William had a contract in his pocket to build the westerly part of it, a job he finished in 1865. Initially, the Parry Sound Road seems to have been projected as the beginning of an ambitious overland route linking southern Ontario with the vital but isolated Upper Great Lakes outpost of Sault Ste. Marie. Construction of this first "Great Northern Road" got under way as early as 1861, when about 30 kilometres leading east out of Sault Ste. Marie were completed. Probably envisioned primarily as a winter road meant to keep communications open outside the navigation season, it was projected to skirt the north shore of Lake Huron before turning south to Parry Sound, then to swing east again to intersect the Muskoka Road near Bracebridge. The 450-kilometre-long exploration line for the Sault–Parry Sound section was completed in the spring of 1865, when land surveyor James W. Fitzgerald and his 15-man crew, working eastward from the Spanish River, emerged from the bush at Parry Sound. Had the Parry Sound end of this road been built, it would have run due north to cross the Magnetawan River just below Wahwashkesh Lake, before trending northwesterly to bridge the lower French River. And had it ever been completed all the way to Sault Ste. Marie, it surely would have merited the tag "Great." However, by the time Fitzgerald and his crew finished blazing its intended path, the government seems to have abandoned the undertaking, or at least put it on hold. Fitzgerald was immediately commissioned to locate a second route out of Parry Sound, this one designed to entice agricultural settlers into the region lying between that port of entry and Lake Nipissing. The first several kilometres of this new route appropriated the Parry Sound–Sault exploration line as far as the vicinity of Waubamik, before swinging eastward. Perhaps the name Great North Road sounded too good to just throw away, or perhaps the planners wanted to retain the option of eventually going all the way to the Sault; anyway, the mantle of the older, bolder endeavour (likely borrowed in the first place from a trunk road of the same name linking England and Scotland) was shifted to the more modest thoroughfare that is the subject of this book.

Barbara Whitmell displays a chert scraping tool she found in the Whitmell potato patch beside the Great North Road. Judged by an archaeologist to date from the late pre-historic period, it lends credence to the story that the road followed an Indian trail.

———◄◊►———

According to legend, the route Fitzgerald marked out for the new Great North Road followed a traditional overland Indian trail between Parry Sound and Lake Nipissing — although the completed road fell short of going that far, terminating instead at Commanda, where it intersected the Rosseau–Nipissing Road. Unfortunately, neither map nor field notes relating to Fitzgerald's survey seem to have survived, but apparently the right-of-way he marked out was the standard one chain, or 66 feet, in width. Construction of the road got under way in 1867, when a crew assembled by contractor William Beatty largely completed work

Andrew Moore drove oxen from eastern Ontario to Parry Sound, helped chop out part of the Great North Road, then claimed a homestead near the future site of McKellar.

Courtesy of Verna Struke

on the first 10 miles. His contract stipulated payment at a rate of $475 per mile, and the following February, he duly billed the government for $4,750. In reporting, in 1868, to Ottawa on the previous season's expenditures and accomplishments, the Department of Crown Lands of the newly constituted Province of Ontario commented that this first leg of the Great North Road "passes for the most part through a fair arable tract of farming lands, and may be extended beneficially to the Magnetawan River...." This assessment had some basis in fact, because where the road negotiated the valley of the Seguin River and its tributary, Portage Creek, the soil consisted of fertile clay and silt loam, much of which continues to be cropped to this day. Eight more miles were duly added in 1868 (under a contract awarded to William Beatty's youngest brother, John, at a rate of $500 per mile), opening the road as far as McKellar.

Also that year, the Department of Crown Lands in Toronto announced that the Township of McDougall, immediately north of Parry Sound, was now open to agricultural settlement, and that the local Crown land agent, John D. Beatty, was ready to record their location claims. Meanwhile, land surveyors continued measuring off additional townships, barely keeping ahead of the influx of settlers. In 1869, when surveyor John Byrne of Kingston, Ontario, and his crew of axemen began laying out the township of Hagerman, some 35 kilometres out of Parry Sound, he found two settlers, named Hart and Hudson, and a third squatter's shanty, measuring "10x12," already established along Fitzgerald's blazed line. Although he noted that a few acres of bush had been "chopped" by these first-comers, no land was yet under cultivation.

On opposite sides of a charming little lake a mile or so short of the southern boundary of Hagerman Township, Byrne would also have noted the rough beginnings of two more homesteads. These belonged to James McKeown and Andrew Moore, recently arrived from Eastern Ontario, whose family names would be prominent in McKellar affairs for generations to come. On hearing in 1867 of free land about to be offered there, the Moores and McKeowns set out for Parry Sound from Pakenham, Ontario, travelling by ox team. The final leg of their journey of several hundred miles was via the Parry Sound Road, making them one of the first immigrant parties to enter that way. At Parry Sound they picked up the beginnings of the Great North Road and wisely stuck with it until they discovered a rare fertile tract surrounding McKeown Lake. In 1974, McKellar elder William McKeown described his grandparents' early experience:

> They drove up, my father and grandfather, just started off and
> drove up. Came up by Toronto, camped in Toronto one night. My
> grandmother was the first white woman that came into this place,
> Mrs. James McKeown. There was nothing here [McKellar]. They
> helped chop the road out between here and Parry Sound, my

father and grandfather helped do that. My father told me that he was the first man that drove a team of horses across this bridge [in McKellar]. My grandmother, she cooked on a fireplace all winter; had no stove when they first came in. That was tough times. There was no money. There was nothing. Armstrongs, they started the mill and the store, and for years all they could get would be an order on the store. You work for them, and they give you an order on the store.

Propelled by a surging demand for the advertised free land, events then moved quickly. In 1870, the Great North Road was completed to Dunchurch, and probably open to some degree beyond that as far as the Magnetawan River at Maple Island, where it seems to have paused to catch its breath. In 1873, Samuel Armstrong of McKellar won a contract to build eight additional miles, at a cost of $500 per mile. Six years later, however, the road evidently had yet to be brought to a state of "permanent improvement" — that is, suitable for summer traffic as well as winter — beyond Maple Island, where it bridged the Magnetawan. In 1876, the editor of the Parry Sound *North Star* pleaded for more government aid to extend the district's roads, pointing out that the leading edge of settlement had now advanced so far into the interior that a barrel of southern Ontario pork or flour

A poster printed in 1871 advertising land newly opened for agricultural settlement. The introduction reads, "Emigrants to the Province of Ontario."

Courtesy of West Parry Sound District Museum

delivered to the Parry Sound frontier, where homesteads were not yet self-supporting in such staples, now cost more than the same commodities landed in England. By about 1880, though, the Great North Road was finally open all the way — roughly 100 kilometres as the ox plods — to where it bridged Commanda Creek to join the Rosseau–Nipissing Road immediately north of the hamlet of Commanda.

Like life-giving sap flowing up the trunk of a maple in springtime, hope-filled migrants, many of them hailing directly from the British Isles, where an economic depression had loosed another wave of emigration, followed closely behind or forged ahead of the road makers. The 100-acre lots fronting on the road were quickly taken up by first-comers, while those who followed spilled over into back lots, confident that access roads would soon be opened along concession lines laid out by the surveyor for that purpose. Taking Hagerman Township, half way up the road, as an example, between 1871, when the land office in Parry Sound

began registering claims there, and 1879, some 90 individuals filed location papers on a total of 18,000 acres. Under the terms of the Free Grants and Homestead Act of 1868, each individual 18 years old or over could claim 100 acres free of charge (subsequently increased to 200 acres for the male head of a family), and purchase an additional 100 acres for 50 cents an acre. Five years after filing a location claim, the homesteader could apply for title, which would be issued subject to certain condition having been met, principally that 15 acres were now cleared of bush and under cultivation, that a dwelling measuring at least 16 by 20 feet had been constructed, and that the land had been continuously occupied during those five years.

------◄○►------

The opening of Parry Sound District to agrarian settlers followed closely on the heels of the start of lumbering east of Georgian Bay, and in the parts opened up by the Great North Road, logging and settlement progressed neck-and-neck — indeed, hand-in-hand. At the same time surveyors were laying out homesteaders' parcels, the government was carving the region into timber berths and inviting bids from lumbermen. Some of the initial work on the Rosseau–Nipissing Road was performed by the Dodge Lumber Company of New York, which had acquired a timber limit embracing hundreds of square miles along the middle reaches of the Magnetawan River, and established its inland depot where the road reached the east end of Ahmic Lake. The government's thinking was that once lumbermen removed the valuable pine trees, the region, now partially stripped of forest, would be readily converted to agricultural purposes. As it happened, lumbering

A government road-building scheme launched about 1855 opened the southern flank of the Precambrian Shield to settlers. About 20 colonization roads, totalling 1,500 kilometres in length, were built, the most westerly being the Great North Road.

Courtesy of Manuel Stevens/Ontario Ministry of Natural Resources

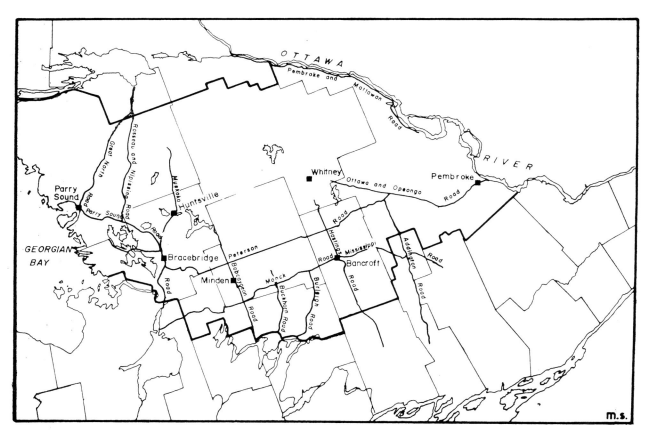

and farming quickly joined in a mutually beneficial partnership. The settlers provided a handy and reliable (compared to the itinerant class of lumberjack) labour force for the lumber camps, and those same camps offered a ready market for oats, which, until a few years of cropping exhausted the soil's reserve of natural fertility, produced bountiful grain crops in newly made clearings. Oats, supplemented by some hay, also purchased from settlers, fueled the teams of horses that transported the timber from stump to riverbank. Thanks to the lumber industry, most of the hundreds of homesteading families that funneled up the Great North Road between 1870 and 1890 managed, by hard work and a good measure of doing without, to keep body and soul together, and in some instances, to achieve a modest degree of prosperity.

Robert Buchanan, who raised a family on a small homestead in the Whitestone community, was typical of the many settlers who earned their main livelihood from working out in the camps and on the river drive. Buchanan would return to his family whenever a weekend found him within walking distance, and Pearl (Buchanan) MacLennan had fond memories of her father's homecomings:

> It was 22 summers that he drove the [Magnetawan] River. Until they got down past Deer [Wahwashkesh] Lake he'd get home sometimes. He'd come home with these tricks. Grab hold of the top of the door and put his chin up to the top. He'd have us all trying these tricks. The broom trick; jumping over the broom handle between your two hands…. Another one was you stood on one leg and held your other foot up behind you, and then you got down and up again without touching anything. You can get down but you can't get up unless you're used to it. Dad learned many songs in the camps, and he would sing them to us on Saturday nights, sitting with his feet toasting under the old high-oven stove after his long walk home. He would strike up a tune and finish it, with his eyes closed, in a long-drawn-out note to end the concert-like evening's entertainment. He just had one horse, and didn't put in much crop. He'd come home and plow the ground for potatoes, and Mother would put them in.

Still, logging and farming bumped heads in certain areas. The flooding of shorelines by lumbermen's dams was a sore point with lakeside settlers. Also, while colonization roads were of no use to lumbermen for moving timber to mill and market — they floated their annual harvests down rivers instead — each autumn they appropriated them to convey supplies to lumber camps in the interior, inflicting wear and tear with their cadge wagons in that wet season. Reporting in 1866, J.W. Bridgland, superintendent of colonization roads for Canada West, observed:

> In scarcely a single instance has any new road we have made had time to settle into a compact state before it has been ploughed into the deepest ruts and mudholes by the heavy provision loads of lumbermen, so that the roads have not only been mainly used by them, but most unfairly made to suffer in their tenderest condition.

Bridgland urged the government to devote part of its timber revenue to maintaining such roads. On the other hand, the lumbermen had a legitimate beef against settlers who allowed fallow fires to escape onto Crown land. As Dan Campbell of Waubamik phrased it, "It was wonderful how much timber was burnt when [settlers] logging it up wasn't careful. Chopping fallows and burning brush, sometimes it would get away and burn a lot of timber. It was bad that way."

To single out one prominent player in the lumbering game, John C. Miller, who in 1875 was elected MPP for Parry Sound–Muskoka under the Liberal banner, happened also to be owner of the Parry Sound Lumber Company, whose water-powered sawmill at the mouth of the Seguin River constituted the region's largest industry. Once elected, Miller immediately began to push for government assistance for a railway linking Parry Sound with the outside — but no railway would come near Parry Sound for another 20 years. He also introduced in Parliament (unsuccessfully) an amendment to the Free Grants and Homestead Act that would allow a locatee to sell his homestead without having completed settlement duties, then claim another free location elsewhere. Miller did, however, have considerable success in wangling government allocations for public works in his riding. The February 6, 1877, edition of the *Toronto Mail* ran a scathing editorial painting Parry Sound–Muskoka as the scene of an unsavoury mixing of "pine and politics," and "a happy hunting ground for political lumbermen, speculators, road-leeches and Grit hacks generally." Not even Parry Sound's revered leading citizen, William Beatty, who "carries with him the Parry Sound vote," managed to escape the *Mail's* wagging finger. Undoubtedly the "road-leech" the newspaper had most in mind was local Liberal organizer Duncan Macdonald, who Miller had just got appointed as local inspector of colonization roads — or "mud-road boss," as the grateful but ever-cynical Macdonald immediately characterized himself. In truth, although roads, railways and waterway improvements certainly aided the lumberman and merchant as much as the struggling settler, the three enjoyed a mutually beneficial working relationship, and together drew the map of the district we know today.

CHAPTER TWO

Carving Out the Route

THE GREAT NORTH Road began its difficult journey just metres from Georgian Bay, near the foot of a steamer dock on the south shore of Parry Sound, the water body, and directly across the Seguin River from Parry Sound, the village. The community on the river's left bank was at first called Carrington, then Parry Harbour, before formally joining Parry Sound at its incorporation in 1887. It was a curiously mixed marriage, for Parry Harbour was "wet," while Parry Sound, occupying land originally patented by temperance advocate William Beatty, was "dry," enforced by a clause in all property deeds forbidding the sale of alcoholic beverages. The amalgamation was vigorously opposed by Parry Harbour hotelier W.F. Thomson, who saw it as a device to put him out of business, but when it happened, Parry Sounders wanting a drink could still find it by crossing the Seguin River bridge and following the Great North Road to its point of commencement.

The same point also marked the terminus of the Parry Sound Road, which in the mid-1860s had provided Parry Sound with regular winter mail and stage service to Bracebridge and the outside world. The Great North Road followed the Seguin upstream for a few hundred metres to just above the first rapids, then bridged the river to parallel the right bank for a short distance before plunging into the unbroken forest. In passing through Parry Sound as it exists today it would have ascended Seguin Street to James Street, and there resumed its appointed northerly course by following James Street and William Street to the town limits near the Mill Lake dam. There it briefly reclaims its identity on today's map, a few kilometres of township road leading to Highway 124 still being sign-posted as the North Road.

The contract under which William Beatty constructed the first 10 miles of the road stipulated a right-of-way cleared 40 feet wide (a narrow avenue through a forest towering a hundred feet or more overhead), while the road itself was to be 14 feet wide, and on hills and sharp corners two feet wider at intervals "to admit the passage of teams." Few words were wasted on what the roadbed was to consist of, so it closely hugged the natural contours of the landscape. Generally, whatever soil was dug out of the ditches sufficed for both fill and surface dressing. Two ditches, each three feet deep and positioned 11 feet from the middle of the road, were expected

"Governor" William Beatty founded the town of Parry Sound and promoted settlement of the district.

Two samples of records kept by Thomas McGown while he oversaw construction of various branch roads sheds light on some of the detail involved.

Courtesy of Jack McGown

to produce an eight-inch crown, but when there was only one ditch, such as where the road skirted exposed bedrock, the government inspector would settle for a six-inch crown. Tree stumps had to be "grubbed" from the actual roadbed but not from the cleared area beyond the ditches (it is said, however, that for many years traffic was forced to flow around both sides of a massive pine stump at Fairholme that proved too formidable for the simple tools of the day). On steep side hills the contractor was instructed to tilt the road surface into the hillside, retaining the outer embankment with "good substantial pine, tamarack, or hemlock logs." The degree of grade of a hill was left to the discretion of the government-appointed road overseer. The most difficult slope Beatty had to contend with was Tug Hill, a kilometre or so south of Waubamik, which, despite frequent streamlining of its profile, continues even today to confront northbound traffic with an abrupt climb.

The contract devoted a good deal of attention to coping with water, in the form of streams, swamps, surface run-off, and mud. Culverts were to be constructed of hewn hemlock, cedar, or tamarack timbers — or as a last resort spruce, which quickly decays in damp situations. Where the road crossed a bog, it was to be more or less floated on a mat of tree trunks laid perpendicular to its course. An eight-foot laneway adzed down the middle would smooth the way somewhat for passing wagons. Vestiges of similar stretches of "corduroy" (or "crosslay" or "crossway") still jar motorists venturing off the beaten path on little-used back roads. The contract also specified how rock quarried from the right-of-way was to be disposed of, but granite being easier to circumvent than penetrate, it is unlikely that much, if any, nitroglycerin or blasting powder was expended on smoothing the path of the original Great North Road. Later, as the road was straightened and leveled under annual allotments of government funds, explosives did come into play, giving rise to the following anecdote. A "deviation" was being made north of McKellar, and when a case of dynamite was delivered to the site, the foreman, unfamiliar with how to employ the new-fangled stuff, asked his gang, "Does anybody here know anything about dynamite?" At this, Irishman Thomas Dickie piped up, "Sure and I do; I know it's dommed dangerous stuff!"

Parry Sound District land fit for cultivation occurs only in scattered patches, the most productive being deposits of clay and silt where once stood post-glacial lakes that later shrank to the dimensions of Manitouwabing and Whitestone lakes, to cite the main examples along the Great North Road. Less productive — although equally attractive to the unwary settler — were occasional level but sandy intervals that relieved the general landscape of bedrock and swamp. As a consequence, the communities that took root and showed some promise of permanence tended to be widely scattered and often well removed from the central artery of the colonization road. People in these isolated settlements soon banded together to petition the government to provide them with better access than the trails they had made themselves, so, as the Great North Road wound its way into the interior it sprouted random branches like an ill-formed tree. Thomas McGown, a woodsman of Scottish birth who settled in Parry Sound (said to be its third white settler) in 1864, blazed out and oversaw the building of some of these ancillary roads. One was the "Mills Road," begun in 1879. This apparently was the route that later became known as the "Pickerel Hills Road," and which branched off the Great North Road midway up Ferrie Township to tap into a promising tract of agricultural land encountered by surveyors laying out townships flanking the Pickerel River. When word of heavy soils around Wauquimakog Lake reached the outside, Scottish and English immigrants rushed in to stake claims and launch a settlement they called McConkey Corners but which officialdom later changed to Loring. This was followed, five years later, by an influx of immigrants from Germany, who would name their community Arnstein. No doubt H.H. Cook, MP for east Simcoe, had a part in getting the Pickerel Hills Road built: the Ontario Lumber Company, of which he was a principal partner, owned a large timber limit in that quarter and had established its inland headquarters in central McConkey Township, a few kilometres northwest of Loring. About this time, a third offshoot settlement, Golden Valley, began taking form further east along the Pickerel River. When, beginning in 1886–87, an east-west artery was opened to allow communication between the three, Thomas McGown was again appointed to blaze out the route and oversee construction.

Even though the frontier had now advanced nearly 100 kilometres beyond Parry Sound, the Parry Sound *North Star* maintained a paternal interest in its settlers. Its issue of August 28, 1879, remarked on one of those:

Thomas McGown arrived in Parry Sound in 1864 and achieved prominence as a road builder and wood ranger.

Courtesy of Jack McGown

> *The first settler in the Township of McConkey will be Mr. James Littlejohn who was in Parry Sound on Tuesday fitting out for his big push northward. He will be accompanied by Mr. J. Bain, and the pair will, after following the new road through Mills [Township] as far as it goes, be compelled to pack in their supplies for a long distance. Mr. Littlejohn reports the land in McConkey equal to any north of Barrie....*

The Pickerel Hills Road was so named out of respect for the precipitous topography it had to negotiate in crossing the Pickerel River. A second distinctive feature was a place where it passed through a tract occupied, before loggers found it, by an exceptionally dense stand of pine. In order for wagons to thread their way through the maze, some larger tree stumps had to be hewn flat on their inner sides. Everett Kirton, a son of Loring's first blacksmith, wryly remarked in his *History of Northern Parry Sound District* that, "The Pickerel Hills Road was well-named as far as the hills part applied, but the word road was a misnomer."

Thomas McGown's field records of his road projects have passed down to his great-great-grandson Jack McGown of Parry Sound. Some pages from those note-books are reproduced here (page 24) to provide a glimpse of what was involved in carving out these branch roads.

DUNCAN FRASER MACDONALD

One of Parry Sound's more prominent early citizens was Duncan Fraser Macdonald (the "mud-road boss" referred to a couple of pages back) who, in a working life spanning nearly 50 years, held such local government posts as Crown Timber Agent, Indian Agent, Inspector of Homesteads, and Inspector of Colonization Roads. A keen and highly opinionated observer of the passing scene with a special flair for scathing invective — he once characterized Sir Sam Hughes, Canada's bumptious Minister of Militia at the outbreak of the Great War, as being "as noisy as an empty threshing machine in a big barn" — his writings provide a colourful account of daily happenings in early times. Between government appointments, Macdonald was constantly on the go cruising timber, prospecting and working on land surveys. He spent much of the winter of 1875–76, for example, employed as the explorer for a survey party locating a right-of-way across northern Parry Sound District for a railway that would never be built, ranging widely on snowshoes by day and sleeping under canvas or cold starlight by night. He left us a record of this and many other wilderness experiences in the pocket diaries he faithfully kept, whether navigating a remote waterway in a birchbark canoe or prowling the halls of political power at Queen's Park. His diary provides a different slant on road building, recording the passing scene as well as the job at hand, thus providing colour that McGown's dry bookkeeping lacks. In the fall of 1892, the Department of Crown Lands handed Macdonald a job supervising road improvements to be carried out on the Great North Road at Maple Island and on a branch leading west toward Whitestone. Local labourers and overseers were hired, and on October 11 Macdonald set up his headquarters in vacant premises belonging to pioneer settler Adam Farquhar, two or three kilometres north of Dunchurch. Following are excerpts from his diary:

> Wednesday Oct. 12: *Fine weather and threatening rain. Jack McGown [a son of Thomas McGown and evidently one of Macdonald's foremen] and I worked all day taking out stone on the road. McGhie, Mortimer and Benson [working]. Charlie Mortimer brought the hay and oats. I paid him $10.40 in full. Tim Sheehan [a prominent lumberman of the day] came along on his way to camp.…*

Parry Sound pioneer Duncan Fraser Macdonald, who is quoted frequently in this book, was a keen marksman, hunter and political activist. He stands second from the left in this photograph taken at the Parry Sound shooting range in 1906. His term as "mudroad boss" was the first of several government posts he would hold over the next 35 years.

Photo: Courtesy of Parry Sound Public Library

Letter: Courtesy of Ontario Archives

Oct. 13: *Worked hard and busy all day. Drove down to Dunchurch in the morning [and] got some things at Beveridge, Johnson and Purvis store. I drove up to [overseer] Montgomery's in the afternoon. He has done good work as far as he has gone.*

Oct. 14: *We done a big day's work on the Post Office Hill.... Young Harrison got married today and went home. Cleminhagen and young Butler started to work in the morning. Mr. Butler and Thos. Farley began at noon....*

Oct. 15: *Went to Dunchurch to get the buckboard repaired and it broke down again on my way back to camp – the same old flaw in the tire. Sent down to the Sound for a couple more stone hammers.*

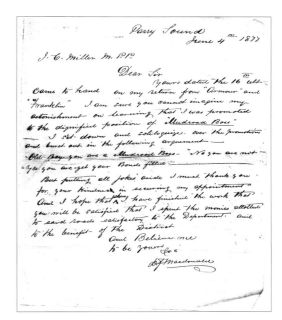

Oct. 17: *The mud froze stiff on the road. Drove down to Dunchurch and got my buckboard fixed up at the Blacksmith shop....*

Oct. 19: *We done big work today. I wired Aubrey White [of the Crown Lands department in Toronto] for the balance of the road money....*

Oct. 20: *I drove down to Dunchurch and got a telegram from Aubrey White re Funds for the Road... I hung out sign [at Farquhar's house] 'The Dog's Nest'.*

Butler's Bridge between Dunchurch and Maple Island.

Oct. 21: *Went down to Dunchurch and met Carey [proprietor of the Dunchurch Hotel] who promised to give me his wagon to fix up Butler's Hill which we made up into first class. We worked hard and done a good day's work.*

Oct. 22: *I got the $300 at Dunchurch for the Road. I met Miller Lawson [a leading light of the now long-vanished "Hardscrabble" settlement, and a political adversary of Macdonald's] at Dunchurch. I got home in the afternoon and paid off some of the men. Wat Leach [probably Walter Leitch, who later became a merchant and community leader in Ardbeg, at the far end of the Whitestone Road] stayed with us all night.*

Oct. 23: *Leach left early in the morning and Benson left through the night some time with his axe and bottle.*

Oct. 24: *I went up to Glenila and paid Montgomery $176.25....*

Oct. 25: *Snow and sleet, dirty weather. Jno. McGown and Robert McGhie drove down from Whitestone with the tools. Jno. Montgomery, Tom Farley, Joe Farley and Cleminhagen went home....*

Oct. 26: *We left the Dog's Nest for home in cold and raw weather. I settled with Carey and got home after dinner which we had at Ball's in McKellar.*

Destined to become the main offshoot of the Great North Road, and ultimately join it in its modern incarnation as Highway 124, was a four-mile-long branch road linking Dunchurch and Ahmic Harbour. The land surrounding this port at the west end of Ahmic Lake was homesteaded by pioneer John Croswell, who laid out a village plot, erected a sawmill and a shingle mill, and established a brickyard, exploiting a clay deposit on the village's outskirts. Beginning in the 1880s and continuing for 40 years, Ahmic Harbour served as both the western terminus for steamboat lines that formed the backbone of central Parry Sound District's transportation system and as the nerve centre for the region's lumbering industry.

CHAPTER THREE

Getting There

IN THE SUMMER of 1865, the supervisor of colonization roads for Canada West, James W. Bridgland, visited Parry Sound to inspect work at the western end of the Parry Sound Road. He found it behind schedule because contractor William Beatty had "laboured under great disadvantages in procuring men owing to his great distance from populous settlements, and the want of any regular and safe communication to the Sound." The Beatty family, Bridgland then noted, was about to rectify the travel problem by launching regular passenger and freight service between Collingwood and Parry Sound using a steamboat then under construction at Thorold, Ontario. This vessel, a wooden-hulled side-wheeler named the *Waubuno,* entered service later that year. During the peak of the Great North Road land rush, most of the homesteaders reached the jumping-off point of Parry Sound by coming "across the water" aboard the *Waubuno.*

The 100-kilometre voyage across Georgian Bay and through the 30,000 Island chain could be an idyllic cruise or an ordeal, depending on season and conditions. Frank Macfie, who sailed the high seas as a marine engineer before coming to Parry Sound, used to say that the only time in his life he was seasick was during his initial crossing of Georgian Bay. But Frank did not heave his breakfast over the rail of the *Waubuno,* for a few months earlier she met her end along the island-studded eastern shore of the Bay. Enroute to Parry sound in November 1879 after sailing the upper Great Lakes for 14 years, she was wrecked on a reef south of Sans Souci, and all 35 passengers and crew aboard perished. In years to come, the handed-down lore of many pioneering Great North Road families would include proud mention of their arrival via the *Waubuno,* and the number of those who supposedly crossed on her last successful trip would be rivaled only by those who, through some fortuitous quirk of fate, missed boarding for that final, fateful voyage. The *Waubuno* is Parry Sound's *Mayflower* and *Titanic* combined in a single wooden hull.

On docking in Parry Sound and leaving behind the relative comfort of a passenger steamer, a party of settlers was now faced with moving themselves and their possessions up the Great North Road. Men who came in ahead to find a location and

The William Beatty Company's steamer *Waubuno* brought the vanguard of Parry Sound settlers across Georgian Bay from the railhead at Collingwood. She was lost, with all on board, in a storm in November 1879.

Courtesy of Dave Thomas

Freight sheds at the steamer dock in Ahmic Harbour in November 1906. The goods being loaded aboard a wagon are destined for a general store, a lumber camp, or perhaps a deer hunters' camp.

Courtesy of John Boyd/National Archives of Canada PA 60918

throw up a shanty usually just hoisted their gear on their backs, easing the burden with a tumpline passing across the forehead. However, a family needed some form of transportation. Some brought cattle with them, one or two of which could be harnessed to a simple sled or jumper for the journey inland, but costly horses were beyond the reach of the average settler (and harder to feed; cattle could subsist on "beaver hay" — wild grasses growing on land once occupied by beaver ponds — or even brush, but horses could not). Most homesteads soon boasted a few cattle, and by the 1880s horses were not uncommon, but at the outset the settler's feet were oftentimes the only means of locomotion he could call his own. (Charlie Quinn used to boast that when, at the age of three, he came with his parents to the Balsam settlement, he walked the 25 kilometres from Parry Sound.) The newcomer with a quantity of goods and chattels to move, and no transport of his own, had to arrange it with someone who had. In many cases this was an enterprising individual named Hugh Gibson, who had arrived in the vanguard of settlement and, after staking out a homestead north of Dunchurch, launched a sideline in the form of "cadging" for those who followed. Nearly a century later, his son Bob would explain how it came about:

> He and his two brothers, Frank and Billy, came from Ireland… to Owen Sound and came across on the boat to Parry Sound. They came up, crossed the narrows in Dunchurch on a log, and came to what would be Concession 13 in Croft [Township]; they squatted on it, the three of them, and built a little shack. From there, my father located over on the [Whitestone] lake shore, in Hagerman…. There was no one else in that area at the time, and the North Road was just an Indian trail, not yet improved. The trail came from the south shore of Lake Nipissing to Georgian Bay…. It crossed [the Magnetawan River] at Markham's Rapids and went on to Lake Nipissing. After people came and started to log, my father worked out one month. The first logs, you see, was cut and hewed in the bush, boat timber to go to England. If a tree [could make a stick] 60 or 70 feet without any knots or any punk in the butt, they'd take it out, sloop it to the river. If it couldn't, they just left that tree and got one that would. Anyway, my father

*worked one month and he got eight dollars. He figured he'd never
make a go of it like that. He got oxen first, and went down and got
stuff and toted up through here. Then he got horses. See, he
moved all the settlers in here.*

The oral histories of many families whose ancestors settled around Maple
Island and beyond begin with a journey up the Great North Road, riding on or
trudging behind Hugh Gibson's wagon or sleigh. He got started by hauling
supplies from Parry Sound for a crew building the road between Dunchurch and
Maple Island. (Gibson liked to tell about an extended "hoot," fueled no doubt by
liquor that arrived in his wagon, that ensued among the workmen upon reaching a
point where the Indian trail dropped over a virtual cliff to ford the Magnetawan
River, halting work. The eventual solution to the impasse was to bridge the river at
Maple Island a short distance downstream). It was a short step from that job to
one of unofficial stage operator, hauling goods and passengers up and down the
road, and cadging supplies to distant lumber camps, an enterprise that led in turn
to purchasing herds of cattle and driving them to the camps for butchering there.
In winter, he cadged from points as distant as the railhead at Gravenhurst, taking
advantage of level going offered by the frozen surface of the Muskoka Lakes.
Gibson, according to his son, was immune to cold:

> *He never wore a sweater till he was 65 years old. He just wore
> long leather boots – real thick cowhide boots, wear for years – and
> no socks. He always stopped at the hotel at McKellar for dinner,
> and they knew what day he'd be coming. There was this traveller
> came in and he had a big fur overcoat on, and gauntlets, and Mr.
> Manning said, "Surely it can't be
> all that cold. There'll be a man
> in here today with a felt hat on,
> and leather boots with no socks
> in them." He wouldn't believe it.
> He said, "If he comes, I'll treat
> the crowd, and if he don't come,
> you'll have to treat them." It
> wasn't very long till my father
> pulled in, and they asked him,
> "Are you very cold, Hughie?"
> "No, it wasn't bad at all." They
> said, "How many socks have you
> got on?" He whipped off his
> leather boot and showed them
> his bare foot. So [the traveller]
> told 'em, "Step up to the bar and
> have drinks before dinner."*

White-bearded
Hugh Gibson,
who in early times
made a business
of "cadging" for
settlers, with
his neighbour
James Hamilton.

Courtesy of
Norman Gibson

In spite of the fact that cadging
took him away from his Whitestone
Lake acreage for extended periods,

Hugh Gibson still managed to turn it into a successful farm. "People would come out from the camps in the spring," his son explained, "and they had no homes, and they had to stay somewhere till the drive started. Two or three of them would stay [at the Gibson homestead] for their board, glad to have a place to sleep and eat, and they'd chop a fallow and help clean up the land."

———————◄○►———————

In spite of the slow pace of travel, traffic accidents were not unknown. Runaways, the most common such occurrence, made the news pages if sufficiently spectacular or if a prominent citizen was involved. An incident reported in the April 25, 1879, edition of the *North Star*, qualified on both counts: "By the running away of his horse on Seguin St., Mr. Joseph Irwin [proprietor] of the Thomson House, Parry Sound, was thrown from his cutter, which was smashed to pieces. Mr. Irwin escaped without injury."

The narrowness of the road inevitably created problems when vehicles met. Rev. W.W. Walker, who assumed the post of Methodist minister in Dunchurch in 1891, describes one such incident in his book *By Northern Lakes*, published in 1896. On a dark night he was driving in his Armstrong cart from Dunchurch to Fairholme for a revival meeting in the little log schoolhouse there. With tongue perhaps only half in cheek, Walker suggested it was a case of his being tested by Satan, who employed "a half-drunken hotel-keeper to run into the preacher's rig with a heavy team and spring wagon, and pile cart, horse and missionary all in a heap in the fence corner." All was made right the following day, however, when Walker, who "recognized the wretch, who at the time [of the accident] was half filled with distilled damnation," exacted a promise of payment for repairs to the dashboard and one wheel of his cart.

What may have been the Great North Road's first "traffic court" case stemmed from an incident part way down Tug Hill, a couple of kilometres south of Waubamik. One winter day, Hugh Gibson and another Dunchurch-area man, John "Happy Jack" Stevenson, both happened to be driving to Parry Sound. In the bar of the McKellar House, where both stopped for lunch, some comparisons were made as to the relative merits of their horses. Stevenson was first back on the road, but Gibson soon caught up, and while descending Tug Hill whipped up his horses and swerved out of the track to pass. In doing so his sleigh caught a corner of Stevenson's jumper, upsetting it and loosing a string of

This ford beside the Jordan Creek bridge near Dunchurch provided teamsters with a convenient place to water their horses.

epithets from its driver. On arriving in Parry Sound, Stevenson found a justice of the peace and laid a complaint against Gibson for failing to share the road. When his summons arrived, Gibson in turn had Stevenson "pulled" for using profane language in public. The court fined Gibson $15 and Stevenson $18, so Gibson boasted he'd won the day. So goes the story according to handed-down Gibson family lore. Stevenson left no offspring, so his version of events is lost to history.

A stopover at Glenila in December 1885.

Courtesy of Parry Sound Public Library

—◄○►—

In its original state, the Great North Road was more a footpath than a thoroughfare for vehicles. Thomas "T" Lundy used to recall the time his father came home from Dunchurch marvelling at how busy it was, "six rigs" having passed through the village that day. The mere passing of a sleigh or buggy was reason to pause and observe. Allan Robertson of Dunchurch told about travelling a back road by sleigh, and passing a small log building with a cluster of children in the yard. When young Allan remarked that it must be a school, his dad said no, it was just a house. There were 18 children in that family, and those of walking age had hurried outside to enjoy the spectacle of a passing team and sleigh.

Centres where goods and services could be had usually lagged far behind the vanguard of settlers, so marathon business trips via "shanks' mare" were the order of the day. A June 1885 edition of the *North Star* noted the arrival in Parry Sound of one Charles K. Arthur of Mills Township, who had "walked the distance of above fifty miles in one day." Bob Gibson spoke of a Mrs. Gorham of Whitestone who "carried wheat on her back, all she could carry, down to the grist mill at McKellar. They'd give her flour and she'd carry it back, before they had bread." Many old-timers spoke of carrying home 100-pound bags of flour on their backs, or dragging them on deerskins. When cattle drovers "drove" their stock to market, they too mostly walked — that is, when not running to prevent a maverick steer from escaping into field or forest bordering the road.

Those with wheels or runners at their disposal found the trip hardly more of a pleasure jaunt, for conditions met with could be hard on both traveller and conveyance. A news report from McKellar dated September 1, 1904, noted the arrival of Albert Creasor's stage "in a broken down condition, so that Mr. Creasor was obliged to proceed on his way in a single rig." Generally speaking, the road was better in winter than the rest of the year. Ice and packed snow smoothed the way and speeded passage considerably, and on top of that, a sleigh carried a greater payload than a wagon. Once well frozen, the district's many lakes offered level paths that bypassed hilly sections and provided short-cuts to back settlements. However, a severe snowstorm could nullify such advantages, and in early winter these came frequently, for the Great North Road lay squarely in the Georgian Bay snowbelt. As long as the Bay remained clear of ice, westerly winds scooped loads of moisture from its surface and staggered inland to dump it in road-clogging snowsqualls. (This was but one more misery heaped upon the unsuspecting homesteader, but the extra snow was a boon to the lumberman, who took advantage of a heavy spring runoff to float sawlogs down even the smallest of creeks). In open country, rail fences bordering the road acted as snow fences, trapping drifting snow in the narrow corridor. Everyone then hoped that someone else would blink first and break the road. Sooner or later, someone with urgent business, or perhaps simply responding to a sense of civic duty, would hitch his team to an empty sleigh and tackle the breast-high drifts. There were snowplows around, V-shaped affairs made of planks, but most of these were in lumber camps far back in the bush. Occasionally, three or four neighbours would pool their teams and undertake to plow a stretch of public road, but placing one's trust in the state of the Great North Road could amount to dicing with fate.

About 1907 a branch of what is now the Canadian National Railway intersected the Great North Road at Waubamik, altering patterns of travel and commerce on the Great North Road.

Courtesy of Ida Waddell

This happened in the mid-1880s to a certain Parry Sound gentleman whose "carnal eye," to quote Parry Sound's chief gossip and scold, Duncan Macdonald, "settled down on his wife's servant," tempting him to hatch a plan for a tryst with the "blooming, bouncing pot-wrestler." The fellow, "a military man, [so] he must be something of a strategist," convinced his wife that she owed her parents, living out beyond McKellar, a visit before spring turned the Great North Road into a quagmire. On the appointed morning he hired a horse and cutter, drew up in front of their home — and announced that a small problem had arisen. Some important documents would be ready for signing at the court-house in a day or two, preventing him from going to McKellar himself. But with luck he had managed to engage a reliable boy to do the driving, and so up the road went the wife and child. However, the horse proved to be skittish, the driver inept, and the condition of the Great North Road very bad. On reaching McKellar and inquiring about conditions beyond, the woman was easily persuaded to turn around and return home, where she arrived around midnight. There she found both husband and servant sound asleep in the latter's room "with a bottle of Brandy and bottle of Wine on the table." And "the way she clawed that girl and scratched the old Captain," Macdonald gleefully concluded, "was a caution to cats."

Along the Great North Road the horse-and-cutter and horse-and-buggy seasons shared the year almost equally. This family has stopped at Buchanan's store in Dunchurch.

Courtesy of George Buchanan

Whether employed by some government department, pursuing his private vocation of wood ranger, or out stumping the district on political matters, Duncan Macdonald himself was a regular traveller of the Great North Road, and his diaries provide a commentary on both the road and the wayfarers he met. The state of the road (which ran by his own door on William Street in Parry Sound) was never the best, and during spring and fall it was often fit neither for "sleighing" nor "wheeling." Following are excerpts from Macdonald's 1894 diary, covering a return trip by buggy to a lumber camp 12 kilometres west of Loring and a good 100 kilometres from Parry Sound.

> Friday Nov. 5: *Cold and raw weather. I left home for McConkey. I got to Ball's [Hotel] at McKellar at half past 6. Road heavy and muddy. The local Orangemen had a supper at Ball's ...Sam Armstrong, Old Moffat, Bob Moffat, Saunders, Old Stewart, Old Ball, Tenycke, Jackson, Neilly, and some more old Rattletraps made up the party.*

> Nov. 6: *Froze hard last night. I left McKellar for Dunchurch at 8 a.m. I met Jno. A. Johnson [a prominent logging contractor who, in his capacity as Crown Timber Agent, Macdonald had frequent dealings with] on his way to Parry Sound. I stayed at Dunchurch and got my horse shod.... The weather looks wintry.*

Nov. 7: Cold and raw. The road frozen hard. I left for Loring at 9 a.m. and got to "Kyle's" [at Loring] at 6 p.m. …. I never drove over…as bad a piece of road as the Pickerel Hills. I shot 2 Partridges and feathered the 3rd.

Nov. 8: Froze hard last night. I drove into Jerry McGuire's camp on Balsam Lake. Got there at 2 p.m. Terrible road….

Parry Sound photographer John Boyd captured this scene, typical of winter travel on the Great North Road, while travelling to Ahmic Harbour in 1912. The pair of telegraph poles reveal that the district is "on line."

Courtesy of John Boyd/National Archives of Canada PA60851

Nov. 13: Snowed all night…about 8 inches of snow fell. I left the camp for Kyle's at 9 a.m. got in at 12 noon. Wheeling very heavy….

Nov. 14: Mild and cloudy. I left Loring for Dunchurch at 9 a.m. Roads heavy and bad wheeling. I fed the horse at the Pickerel River and drove on and reached Dunchurch at 7 p.m. No sleighing and heavy wheeling and Rough roads on horseflesh.

Nov. 15: I left Dunchurch for home at 10 a.m…. I got home at 3 p.m. No sleighing on this… side of Dunchurch.

With his frequent expeditions to the northern reaches of the district, Duncan Macdonald would become more intimately familiar with the full length of the Great North Road than perhaps any other individual. On one occasion his horse left him stranded along the road's most remote stretch. Deciding to camp at "The Burned Bridge" on the Pickerel River while doing some timber cruising in the vicinity, he tied up his hired steed, only to have it break loose and escape in the night. When the job was finished, a week later, he had to walk down to the Cataract Hotel at the Ferrie River, and there hire another rig to take him to Dunchurch, the home of the escaped horse — which had yet to show up at its stable. In addition to his diaries and letters, Duncan Macdonald left a valuable photographic legacy. Some views captured by his cumbersome glass-plate camera are the earliest known of the Great North Road.

◄○►

Respite from the preceding pages, which paint a generally miserable picture of early travel on the Great North Road, is found in a passage from a letter quoted in Rev. John Firmin's *God's Country*. Written in 1876 by an unnamed woman newly arrived in Spence Township, to a sister in England, it reveals that on a sunny day in early autumn, when the road was dry and the air free of biting insects, the journey up from Parry Sound could actually be a pleasant experience:

As you are aware from my last letter we have now been here nearly two months, but if I live to be an hundred I shall never forget the array of colour that greeted us on our trip. Indeed I have seen many masterpieces of colour, painted by famous artists, but believe me my dear sister God is still the greatest artist of them all. He spared not one colour in His vast repertoire… The maples had been touched by frost and the leaves had taken on different colours from gold to blood red and all the possible, and perhaps impossible, shades in between. These stately trees reach their branches over the road as if to have a more personal contact with their neighbours across the street. To ride or walk between this avenue of colour makes one feel as if their life is receiving an additional blessing from the Almighty…As much as I love the home land, I have come to love this vast land of Canada even more…"

Parry Sound District abounded in lakes, many of them supporting populations of such desirable fish as trout and pickerel. Sportsmen from outside would soon learn this and ascend the Great North Road armed with fishing rods. The settlers, though, fished not for fun but for subsistence, by spearing on shallow-water spawning beds or gillnetting in deeper water, and using rowboats or birch-bark canoes to get around. Jim Canning, who arrived in McKellar as a child in the 1870s, remembered a vessel of another type:

The first railway to serve Parry Sound was lumber baron John R. Booth's Ottawa, Arnprior & Parry Sound Railway, which was completed to the deepwater port of Depot Harbour on Parry Island shortly before the close of the 19th century. Rose Point, accessed by a four-kilometre steamer or stage ride, became the town's rail passenger terminal.

Courtesy of Ontario Archives

Grand Trunk Station, Rose Point, Ont.

*This fellow used to do a bit of toting on Manitouwabing Lake,
used to bring lime and stuff up [to McKellar] from where he lived
[Hurdville]. Had a big dugout canoe about 20 feet long. It could
hold, I guess, a couple of ton of stuff. Had a little windlass, like,
and he'd pull up this sail, and he'd come along. Not very fast, but
he'd come; come all the way up from where the Seguin leaves
Manitouwabing Lake. He'd come up to McKellar, and take back
provisions and one thing and another for anybody that wanted it.*

In 1883, Duncan Macdonald heralded an improvement in communications
with the interior:

*The Muskoka Inland Navigation Co. are going to build a snug
little steamer this winter and will run her from John Croswell's
[at Ahmic Harbour] to Dodge's old Depot [Port Anson on the
Nipissing Road] where she will meet the Rosseau stage daily,
then running on to Magnetawan village for Burks Falls carrying
the mail. Passengers leaving Toronto for Burks Falls will reach
there with a drive of 28 miles from Rosseau, whereas now they
have 44 miles without counting the steamboat run from Port
Sydney to Huntsville.*

With the arrival in Burks Falls, in 1885, of the Northern & Pacific
Junction Railway, Ahmic Harbour became a busy shipping port and passenger
terminal for communities along the middle reaches of the Great North Road.
During the navigation season, a watershed formed just below Dunchurch,
with those living north of that imaginary line coming and going via Ahmic

Harbour and Burks Falls, and those to the south continuing to use Parry Sound as a way outside. Rev. W.W. Walker entered the district via Burks Falls in 1891, when coming to Dunchurch to take a preaching charge there. The book he later wrote recalled highlights of the adventure, beginning as the steamer threaded its way through the locks at Magnetawan, between Cecebe and Ahmic lakes:

> A Toronto gentleman wearing a tall and very glossy silk hat, was sitting just in front of the pilot-house, when the mast, which the sailors had forgotten to lower, caught the telegraph wire, giving the bowsprit a sharp jerk, and tilting it backward with considerable force, so as to alight squarely on the crown of our Toronto friend's beautiful castor, which it crushed beyond recognition... also wounding the head slightly.... The captain...very honourably paid him for the plug....

> Soon we were in sight of Ahmic Harbour. A neat-looking little place with a nice new frame church.... Also, the village contained an hotel, which was soon to give place to a very large one, veneered with brick..., a blacksmith's shop, carpenter and paint shop and several private dwellings.... As we landed we observed a few men loitering lazily around. They looked as though they had quarreled with work years ago, and had never again made up friends. After some little delay in adjusting luggage, we took our seats in the stage, which was but an ordinary spring wagon with brakes attached — no doubt for the purpose of adding dignity to the vehicle, as there were no hills to amount to much on the road to be traversed. The driver said it

The steam yacht *W.B. Armstrong* on Lake Manitouwabing in 1892. Three years later, when it was sold to a buyer in Parry Sound, the machinery was removed and the hull was sawn in two for transport by road.

Courtesy of Parry Sound Public Library

When rail service finally reached downtown Parry Sound, in 1906, a crowd gathered across the Great North Road to welcome the first passenger train.

Courtesy of Parry Sound Public Library

was but four miles to Dunchurch...but... the miles appeared tremendously long.... At last, however, as we passed over the brow of a bluff, we had a splendid view of the village, which was to be our home for two years.

The first steamboat on the Great North Road proper was S&J Armstrong's *Ada*, launched on Lake Manitouwabing in 1881 to tow sawlog booms and perform general transportation duties. In 1885, the Armstrongs floated the idea of moving the *Ada* overland to Ahmic Lake, on the Magnetawan River, to take advantage of new opportunities in the transportation field. They had been logging on the middle Magnetawan for a number of years, and now locks were being installed at Magnetawan village, opening up a navigable stretch of water extending all the way to Burks Falls. Sketchy records mention a small steamer called the *Ada* working on Ahmic Lake around that time, so evidently the plan was carried out. But if the enterprising Armstrongs had visions of opening a steamship line on the Magnetawan they soon surrendered the field to others, principally the Muskoka Navigation Company. A year or two later, the Armstrongs purchased the steam yacht *Aeriel* from the Parry Sound Lumber Company, intending to use it in their lumbering operations at McKellar. The Thompson sawmill, which succeeded the Armstrong enterprise at the turn of the century, launched a third vessel, the *Irene,* on Lake Manitouwabing, and it may have been the last steamer to ply those waters. Lumbermen also used steam-powered craft on Shawanaga, Whitestone and Wahwashkesh lakes during the pine logging era.

WAYFARERS

"Lots of shanty tramps on the road," Duncan Macdonald told his diary on October 13, 1891. Macdonald was then overseeing improvements to the Great North Road around Maple Island, and the passing parade he referred to consisted of men on foot seeking work in one or another of the numerous lumber camps operating in the Magnetawan and Pickerel river watersheds to the north. If turned down at one camp (or dissatisfied with the food), the itinerant shantyman would simply shoulder his "turkey" and continue his march into the wilderness. Turkey was the accepted name for the grain sack in which he carried spare clothing, tobacco and other comforts that might, if he was musical, even include a violin or a harmonica. Writing in the history series *Along Memory Lane with Hagerman People,* Whitestone-born Pearl MacLennan, who as a child often witnessed her father leaving for the camps, recorded a curious detail about the lumberjack's turkey. The sack was slung over his shoulder and held in position by a short length of harness strap or piece of rope tied to top and bottom. The loose top of the sack presented no problem, but a knot tied to a bottom corner was liable to slip off. The solution, Pearl remembered, was to first push a medium-sized potato into that corner. One wonders how often the potato got eaten when the shanty tramp was caught between camps at mealtime.

Also called tramps were the unemployed men who, in the Great Depression of the 1930s, trudged up and down the road looking for casual employment and their next meal. Generally poorly dressed and often unwashed, they were emissaries from a wider world beyond my horizons who I viewed with both apprehension and curiosity. One Sunday morning in the summer of 1936, a man aged about 30 knocked on our back door and asked if he might be spared something for breakfast. But first, he tendered his thanks for his sleepover in our haymow. Had he asked permission the night before he likely would have been offered a bed somewhere, but not in the barn, for farmers placed hoboes, most of whom smoked, right up there with lightning and damp hay as sure causes of barn fires. This man evidently made a good impression on my mother, though, for after breakfast she produced her autograph book and invited him to leave his name and a parting word. His message, pencilled in a hand that skips across the page as if tuned to the lilting rhythm of that ancient compendium of wisdom, was this passage from the *Rubaiyat:*

> The worldly hope men set their hearts upon
> Turns ashes; or it prospers and anon
> Like snow upon the desert's dusty face
> Lighting a little hour or two, is gone.

Hope, in those times, was about the only thing some people had left. K.A. Webster, whoever he was, then shouldered his meager belongings and resumed his tramp up the Great North Road.

While the outbreak of war in 1939 may have precipitated the end of the Great Depression, it hardly diminished the flow of strangers past our door. When word of construction of a huge munitions plant at Nobel, near Parry Sound, reached Northern Ontario, it loosed a flood of job applicants, many of whom could not afford the price of public transportation. One evening in the spring of 1941, a pair of transients came to our door looking for a meal and a place to sleep. One was a slightly built French-Canadian, the other a tall Swiss or German who introduced himself as Joseph Goring, getting himself off on the wrong foot from the beginning, for at that moment in history the name Goring was right up there with Hitler in the pantheon of world-class villains. It very quickly became apparent that our Goring did have a sinister side, for soon after the pair (who had fallen in together not far up the road) were shown upstairs to our spare room, sounds of a scuffle and a heated argument were heard below. In the exchange, Goring, who had attacked his roommate seemingly because he refused to say his prayers, bit him on the hand, causing it to bleed profusely. After my mother bound up his wound, the victim fled our house and found refuge with our nearest neighbour to the south, leaving us with what we believed to be a raving lunatic on our hands. My father finally phoned the police, and after another decidedly uneasy hour, two officers arrived from Parry Sound to conduct the deranged Mr. Goring away.

The transient parade, however, did not let up. In a letter written a couple of weeks later to my oldest brother, who was away in the air force, my mother ruefully wrote,

> Had a 17 yr. old fellow in for Sunday night, worse luck. It was
> raining a little and I did hate to take him in, and sheets etc.
> to wash for him. I wish they would pick on somebody else.
> Mr. Cooke [the United Church minister] says maybe they have
> put a mark on the mailbox. If so, I had better find out the
> "cross dog" and "cranky woman" signs and put them on.

For a while, Ojibways from Parry Island Reserve appropriated the Great North Road as a route to hunting grounds in the interior — treading in the footprints of ancestors, if the road truly did followed an Indian trail. Later came Parry Island people with handicrafts to sell to the settlers. Notable among these were Mr. and Mrs. John Manitouwaba, who in winter ranged as far north as Dunchurch, pulling their supply of baskets on a toboggan and trading a choice item in exchange for lodging wherever night found them.

Mr. and Mrs. John Manitouwaba of Parry Island sold baskets up and down the Great North Road. These examples were purchased from the elderly couple when they came pulling their sleigh load of wares through Sunny Slope in the 1920s.

More common were the peddlers who, carrying packs on their backs (or, later, driving buggies and cutters, and, briefly, even automobiles), made regular rounds of the homesteaders' clearings and lumber camps. Some were "dry goods men" selling clothing, dressmaking supplies and assorted notions. Others offered patent medicines and household needs, while yet others specialized in watches and costume jewelry. Olive (Simpson) Lamb recalled a peddler who,

during her childhood in the 1920s, called regularly at their home on Farley's Road near Dunchurch:

> *Do you remember Mr. Haddad? He used to travel around with an enormous pack on his back, and carrying another in his hand. He was rather short and dark with a heavy moustache, and wore old fashioned, European style clothing, a very quiet, gentle person. He started out in Parry Sound and always came in our sideroad at least once each summer. He stayed with Joe Whitmell's a lot — they were good with peddlers. And Mr. Haddad enjoyed a cup of tea. He kept a very neat pack of good merchandise. He would open it on the floor and hold up things and say, "Shirts for the men, panties for the ladies, toys for the kiddies." He may have had medicines too, but we always bought our medicines from the Rawleigh man.*

One peddler who ranged less widely and limited his stock to a single item was John Foote — better known as "Gatling Gun" for the potency of his product. He was a hermit who concocted a physic in his hut, put it up in whisky bottles, and sold it from door to door between McKellar and Dunchurch. He sometimes carried a concertina and entertained the housewife with a tune before launching his sales pitch.

Crafts people included sharpeners of knives and saws, and commercial photographers who, often riding a sleigh pulled by a pair of dogs, journeyed to lumber camps to line up the inhabitants for a group photo, and take orders for prints costing the lumberjack three or four days' wages. Travelling salesmen making the rounds of country stores also warrant mention, although they, a cut above the common peddler, generally hoisted their sample cases aboard the stage and rode in style.

These Dunchurch scenes, captured a couple of years apart, mark a major transition in modes of transport. About 1927, one of a pair of hitching posts that had long stood in front of Buchanan's store was replaced by a shiny new gasoline pump.

Courtesy of Gordon Powell

Increasing automobile traffic and the Second World War saw the brief appearance of yet another form of foot traveller, the hitchhiker. Then, in the post-war era, automobiles became commonplace, and hardly anyone walked anymore.

◄○►

Its perennially poor condition, combined with a scarcity of people who could afford them, kept the Great North Road largely free of motorcars for the first decade or two of the automobile age. However, the post-war boom of the 1920s, although muted by topography and distance, penetrated deeply enough into the hinterland to admit a trickle of economy cars such as the Model T Ford, the Star and the Essex.

Worth noting is a steam-driven automobile that, in an early version of a manufacturer's road test, took on the challenge of the Great North Road and its rough-hewn branches. Whether the contraption "roared," as that decade is said to have done, or merely puffed its way up hill and down dale, its passage clearly impressed some of the citizenry. To the amazement of everyone in Ardbeg, when it steamed into that end-of-the-road metropolis it charged undeterred through the sawdust- and slab-littered yard of the local sawmill. Back down the road at Dunchurch, lumberman Jim Canning, one of that community's rare individuals in a position to invest money, was so taken with how briskly it negotiated the steep slope of the Grange Hill that he signed up for shares in the company manufacturing the vehicle. Quite likely this was the same promotional event that in 1923 persuaded farmer Percy Sword, at Maple Lake Station east of Parry Sound, to ante up $120 for 10 shares in Brooks Steam Motors Ltd., manufacturers of "steam-driven pleasure cars." All that succeeding generations of Swords now have to show for the venture are copies of the company prospectus and Percy's subscription agreement.

Automobiles, such as these in front of Buchanan's store in Dunchurch, became a common sight in the 1920s.

Courtesy of Gordon Powell

For the first couple of decades, motoring would remain pretty much a seasonal thing. At the approach of winter, cars were driven into sheds and jacked up on blocks to give overworked tires and springs a well-earned rest. At the same time, sleighs and cutters were hauled out, and Great North Road traffic resumed its original pace.

The Great Depression left its mark on the road through a massive make-work initiative launched by the Province in 1931, involving the upgrading of public thoroughfares. Local unemployed men were apportioned two or three days of work weekly, and tent camps were set up — one was located at Waubamik, another at Fairholme — to house additional scores of men brought in from southern Ontario. Crews widened lengthy stretches of the road, mostly by digging new ditches and shovelling the earth into the old ones, and here and there a "deviation" was launched through rock and bush to eliminate a particularly crooked section. As a make-work project, it achieved its goal. Earth was excavated with grub-hoe and shovel, and rock was drilled for blasting by men wielding sledgehammers. The job was also fraught with politics. Lyle Jones of Parry Sound, who clerked for a gang of 100 men camped at Waubamik, explained, "I got on because I was a Conservative. The man that gave me a boost was [local Department of Highways superintendent] Ross Miller. I was there all that fall and winter, then in the spring the government changed. Three days after it changed, I came out of there and another man took over." Up at Fairholme the plum job of camp cook similarly changed hands overnight. Subsequent realignments, widenings and levellings of the road have long ago by-passed or buried the modest achievements of this undertaking, but at the time it did noticeably smooth the way for both the travelling public and hundreds of jobless men and their families.

A unique feature of Great North Road traffic during the latter 1930s and the 1940s was the Magnetawan Transfer, an express service operated by Stan Wurm. Driving a mid-size stake truck, Wurm shuttled freight and express between Burks Falls and Parry Sound. Each Friday morning (sometimes a Tuesday trip was added to the schedule), he left Magnetawan for Parry Sound, dropping off stuff at village stores and farm gates, and picking up cans of cream and other farm produce for delivery to customers in town or to a railway express office. By late afternoon, the truck was loaded with a new assortment of goods for the back-haul. What set "The Transfer" apart from ordinary delivery services was that it also

Until the 1940s, when regular snow plowing was instituted, automobiles were put up on blocks for the winter. Stretching the season involved nightly draining of the radiator, difficult starting, tire chains and the risk of getting stuck in a snowdrift.

In the severe winter of 1942-43, during which snowfall totaling over 15 feet was officially recorded at Parry Sound, snowplows struggled to keep even one lane open for workers travelling to the Nobel munitions plant. This picture was taken in Sunny Slope, notorious for its snowdrifts.

Courtesy of Edith Macfie

provided Great North Road residents with a rough-and-ready but free bus service at a time when even the few people who had cars might lack the gasoline or tires to operate them. To catch a ride into town a passenger had only to hang around where he expected Wurm would have a pick-up or drop-off, climb in the back, and find a seat on a bag of feed or a case of canned goods. The ride might be shared with up to a half dozen others, usually all men and boys (the rare woman who turned up was gallantly offered space in the cab). On a fine summer day it was an open-air experience; otherwise, the stake rack was roofed with a tarpaulin. To arrange a return ride, it was necessary to ask where the last stop in town was likely to be and arrive there in late afternoon prepared to wait, for Wurm's schedule was highly flexible.

A couple of my brothers and I rode the Magnetawan Transfer a number of times, usually with some urgent matter such as having an aching tooth pulled as the primary purpose. However, for country boys for whom Parry Sound was practically the edge of the known world, each expedition was an adventure to be remembered. On returning from his first such expedition, about 1937, my oldest brother brought his purchases — a plastic cap pistol and a package of ten Legion brand cigarettes — out to our sugarbush to relieve the tedium of long evenings spent finishing off batches of maple syrup. Sixty-five years later, the musty odour of Bakelite or a whiff of sweet Virginia tobacco smoke still conjures up a vision of sap kettles simmering in the close-pressing, owl-ridden midnight blackness. It was on my own first Magnetawan Transfer adventure that I first tasted beer. Returning from Parry Sound, the truck stopped to deliver several cases of beer to a small house a couple of miles north of town (the nearby Nobel munitions plant was then operating and Parry Sound was booming, so perhaps the recipient was a bootlegger). When we finished piling off the cases, the householder ripped one open and handed a sample to each of the three of us (Wurm, a second free-rider and me). I manfully accepted the green bottle of Black Horse Ale but found the contents so disgustingly bitter that I disposed of most it by surreptitiously decanting it into the grass as I leaned against the doorjamb. I don't recall ever paying for a Transfer ride; seemingly all that was expected in return was help loading and unloading stuff along the way. Whether he saw it that way or not, in providing free rides Stan Wurm performed a vital community service, particularly in wartime when gasoline and tires were in short supply.

In the latter part of the 1930s, the provincial government began attempting to keep the road open to automobile traffic in winter, but the ineffective snow-handling equipment of the day, combined with the wounded state of the economy, made it a hit-and-miss affair. It took another historic event, the Second World War, to bring about regular snow plowing. In 1940, a huge munitions works was built (literally on the foundations of a First World War facility of the same kind) at Nobel, near Parry Sound, and at peak production it employed 4,000 shift-workers, many of whom commuted to work via the Great North Road. Around-the-clock road traffic now being essential to the war effort, ways were quickly found to accommodate it. The road was plowed regularly throughout winter, and one year, when the spring thaw turned sections between McKellar and Dunchurch into quagmires, teams of horses were marshalled to tow stuck vehicles. On April 15, 1941, my mother wrote in a letter to my brother in the air force:

> *Roads are terrible…. 4 or 5 teams are kept harnessed & men stay*
> *awake overnight to help any in trouble. I just saw a car nearly*
> *over in the ditch, on the left going down. They scoot all over the*
> *road to find the best track. They are piling on gravel and shoveling*
> *but still it is bad.*

In fact, the author of this book was one of those teamsters who soldiered in the mud of the home front to help keep Nobel's cordite, guncotton and TNT production lines rolling.

———◄○►———

Once his immediate needs were reasonably well taken care of, the homesteader had time to think about such extra creature comforts as improved lines of communication. In the spring of 1879, a petition was raised around McKellar for daily mail service from Parry Sound. The message seems to have reached a favourable government ear, for shortly thereafter a newspaper report stated that a vehicle "intended for the McKellar mail stage" was currently under construction at Whitchello's wagon and carriage shop in Parry Sound. Mail stages of the time customarily doubled as carriers of people. "Quinn's stage" was one of the earliest to operate on this route. In very early times, mail came to Dunchurch only once a week, sometimes borne on the back of mail carrier Arthur Millin. The first regular Parry Sound–Dunchurch stage service is said to have been that operated by a Mr. Junck of McKellar. About 1890, this route was taken over by Albert Creasor, one of whose daughters, quoted in *Along Memory Lane with Hagerman People,* left us this account of her father's work:

Stage operator Albert Creasor passing northbound through McKellar. This trip also served as a honeymoon excursion for himself and his bride, Hannah Sands. A few kilometres further up the road, he dropped Hannah off at the Sands farm while he completed his scheduled run to Dunchurch.

Courtesy of Ethel North

John "Daddy" Cox ran the mail from Dunchurch to Maple Island and Whitestone in a dilapidated democrat in summer, and a cutter in winter.

Courtesy of
Bunty Croswell

When quite a young man, Albert contracted with the government to drive the mail stage from Parry Sound to Dunchurch and from Dunchurch to Burks Falls, a distance of about 60 miles. This was before either railway or motorcars were seen in this area, and the mail, passengers and supplies were picked up by Mr. Creasor, who drove a team of horses harnessed to a democrat with a fringed top. The route required two teams of horses and two drivers, so my father took up residence in Dunchurch and operated the Temperance Hotel and ran a livery stable as well as drive the mail stage. For this arduous work he received the magnificent sum of five dollars a day…. Out of this he had to hire an extra driver, buy his horses and all the necessary equipment, as well as pay for lodging and meals for himself and his driver on their stopovers in Parry Sound and Burks Falls. Two of them would leave Dunchurch on Monday morning at 7:00, my dad starting for Parry Sound, stopping at McKellar for dinner, and reaching Parry Sound about 4:30 in the afternoon. The other driver…, whose name was Danny [Cornwell], left Dunchurch at the same time, stopping at Magnetawan for dinner and reaching Burks Falls around 4:30.

His passengers would remember Creasor as a sometimes prickly but generally good-natured fellow, who kept them entertained with a lively line of patter directed at them and his horses in turn. A knack for humouring passengers was a valuable asset, for under the best of conditions it was hardly a pleasure jaunt. James McAvoy remembered the day, in 1889, when he first caught the Dunchurch stage. Conditions were so bad some of the six passengers had to dismount and walk up Tug Hill near Waubamik, and it took all day just to reach McKellar.

Notable among the mail carriers working beyond Dunchurch was John "Daddy" Cox, a tall, grey-bearded and abrasive old-timer who in the early 20th century made thrice-weekly trips by buggy and cutter to Maple Island and Whitestone, and between times acted as caretaker for the schoolhouse situated near his home in Dunchurch. Daddy Cox contributed much to the body of Dunchurch folklore, one example of which will suffice here. It seems one day he was engaged to plow a field, one end of which bordered on the Sunny Slope schoolyard, and every few minutes as he worked, morsels of the salty language he directed at the horses came wafting in the schoolhouse windows. The teacher stormed across the road to a nearby farmstead and demanded that the man of the house do something about the situation, which he did by diplomatically persuading Daddy to save his choicest epithets for the far end of the furrow.

Lumber camps, too, required mail service, and when the Ontario Lumber Company established its inland depot in McConkey township, some 12 or 15 kilometres beyond Loring, a young man named Albert McCallum was engaged to carry the mail between there and Dunchurch, the nearest post office. Everett Kirton's book *History of Northern Parry Sound District* describes the weekly round of this pioneer courier:

> He would leave the depot camp in the northern part of McConkey Township in the morning, and have dinner at Glenila, thence go to Dunchurch, pick up the mail and any other small necessities (usually about 50 pounds) and return to spend the night at Glenila, travelling a distance of 62 miles. He would leave Glenila the next morning arriving back at the depot camp at noon, another 35 miles…. While making this 100 mile trip, he would not walk over a couple of miles. He had a lope that carried him at wonderful speed, and he never seemed to tire.

Mailmen are said either to "carry" the mail or to "run" it, but Albert McCallum did both. Soon, he would turn his boundless energy to the business of lumbering. From the 1890s until the pine ran out, around 1920, he contracted woods operations for lumber companies holding timber limits in the Shawanaga and Magnetawan river watersheds, becoming something of a legend in that field as well.

Henry Moffat, shown here with his wife, Frances Jemima, came from Ireland to Smiths Falls, Ontario, in 1847, and 20 years later moved on to McKellar. He opened a general store, and in 1886 got himself appointed postmaster, founding a dynasty that would endure until 1967, when his grandson Leonard Moffat ended his term of office. One of its first settlers, Henry Moffat was active in McKellar's economic and political affairs throughout his life. Liberal organizer Duncan Macdonald marveled to a friend after running into Moffat in 1911 at the Parry Sound Fair, "Aged 94 years, and if they give him his gruel regular he will vote Tory when he is an hundred."

Courtesy of John Moffat

Leonard Moffat, grandson of Henry, opens the daily mailbag as Norman Whitmell waits for his mail.

The job of village postmaster was something of a political plum, and thus was vulnerable to the political winds. In 1886, however, there was launched in McKellar a dynasty of postmasters that would endure for 81 years. Initially, the brothers S&J Armstrong had the McKellar post office in their store, but during Conservative Sir John A. Macdonald's second reign in Ottawa, the lectern-like pine box containing all the working parts of a post office of the time was carried a stone's throw across the bridge to the premises of Henry Moffat, a storekeeper by profession and a diehard Conservative by political persuasion. Born in Ireland around 1818, Henry came to Canada with his wife, Frances, and their three eldest children in 1847 (a time when thousands of Irish were fleeing famine), settling for a while around Smiths Falls, Ontario, before joining the vanguard of colonists ascending the Great North Road. Henry, who died in 1912 at age 95, was succeeded as postmaster by his son Richard, upon whose death in 1931 Henry's grandson Leonard Moffat assumed the post until his retirement, at age 65, in 1967, Canada's centennial.

John Moffat, great-grandson of Henry, displays the pine box and contents that down through the years constituted the working parts of the McKellar post office.

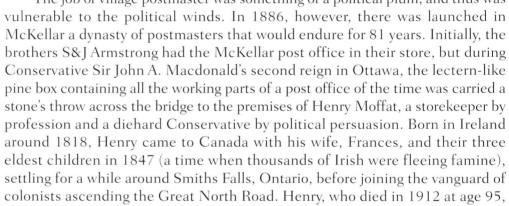

Parry Sound got wired to the outside world prior to 1880, by means of a telegraph line following the Parry Sound Road from Bracebridge. By the early 1890s, service was extended north to McKellar, Dunchurch and Ahmic Harbour, employing terminals installed in general stores at these points. It was both an honour and an opportunity for advancement in life, for a clerk to be assigned by the storekeeper to learn the code and master the cutting-edge art of telegraphy. It was the chance to learn telegraphy that, in 1903, induced young Willis Kenney to come north to Dunchurch to take a position in William Roberston's store. Some photographs Kenney took there appear in this book.

Then, in 1921, the telephone joined the march of progress up the Great North Road. In that year, the McKellar Municipal Telephone System was formed, serving subscribers living as far north as Dunchurch and on various sideroads. Jim (James L.) Moore, who was engaged to manage the enterprise, looked after the many miles of lines, while his wife, Florence, handled the accounts and the switchboard, installed in their home. Mrs. Moore proved to be fully as reliable and durable as the McKellar Municipal Telephone System itself, providing unfailing operator service for over 40 years, until 1963, not long before the system was taken over by Bell Canada.

The McKellar telephone network consisted of several party lines, each serving a number of subscribers having their own "ring": for example, two long rings followed by three short ones. To reach someone on a different line, or make a long-distance call, the caller had to first ring Mrs. Moore, who announced herself with an abrupt "Central!" then performed the necessary cross-plugging of wires. However, subscribers on the same line could ring each other directly, after first lifting the receiver to ensure the line wasn't already in use. The equivalent of dialing "911" in an emergency was one very long ring, by the end of which all within hearing would have lifted their receivers to learn whose house or barn was on fire. Then the volunteer fire department — that is, everyone within hearing — rushed to the scene to render assistance.

In the 1940s, McKellar's communication with the outside world depended on mail delivery man Billy Moore, postmaster Leonard Moffat, and telephone lineman Jim Moore.

Courtesy of John Moffat

"Listening in" on others' conversations was officially frowned upon (when Mrs. Moore detected people thus abusing the system she summarily dispatched them with a gruff "Get off the line!") but widely practiced. Before radio and television, this was how news and gossip, and even vital information were disseminated. We have Joseph "Little Joe" McEwen of Fairholme to thank for the following party line anecdote dating from the 1930s. Bob Farley's farm was a short distance in Farley's Road, while Marshall Dobson, a bachelor, lived on a dead-end branch farther in the same road.

Jim and Florence Moore who, beginning about 1920, between them operated the McKellar Telephone System.

Courtesy of Evelyn Moore

Three or four fellows on Line Twelve had made it up that, in the fall when one of them thought it was time for a feed of [out-of-season] venison, he would phone around and say, "What do you say we go pickin' cranberries today?" Then the one with a hound would turn it loose at his end of the bush, and the others would sneak out to their watches to wait for a deer. Well, one morning I heard Marshall Dobson's ring on my phone, so I picked up the receiver to listen in. It was Bob Farley, all excited. "Oh, is that you, Marshall?" Bobby yelled. Then he says, "Oh, say, Marshall, I just seen three cranberries walkin' in your road!"

CHAPTER FOUR

House and Home

JOE NORTH, WHO arrived with his parents at their homestead at the north end of Whitestone Lake in 1872, when he was eight years old, would remember sleeping under the wagon that brought them there from Parry Sound, with blankets draped around for walls. This served as shelter until a shanty, the first home of most settlers, could be built. This was a simple log structure roughly 12 feet square, a shelter that could be thrown up very quickly using the trunks of small trees for walls and "scoops," overlapping troughs made of split and hollowed-out cedar logs, for the sloping shed roof. Cracks were chinked with moss or daubed with moistened clay. Usually, the man or men of the family arrived ahead in order to have this shelter ready when wife and children came — as did Arthur Millin of Mount Forest, Ontario. Here is how his daughter Mary remembered those difficult first months of homesteading:

In September 1870, my father moved to Parry Sound, and leaving mother and the rest of us there, he came north to look up a homestead. The land was nearly all located up to the "narrows" where the Whitestone [River] crosses the road at Dunchurch, so father crossed and took the next lot and built a little shanty for us to live in the first winter. This done he went back to Parry Sound and hired teams and moved us up…then we moved into our little home with the great trees towering over it [and] like the "bear" we denned up for the winter. As there were no teams to keep the road open, travelling had to be done on snowshoes. I remember hearing of some of the settlers tramping all the way to Parry Sound for flour and groceries, which they drew up on deerskins…. One morning in November we were surprised on waking to find one corner of our shanty raised up about a foot above the ground. So father went out to see what was the matter; he found he had one corner of our shanty on the root of a big birch, which was leaning away from the

Pioneer log homes commonly lived on to serve as extra barns when the owners moved up to frame homes. This one is on the Tully homestead in the Balsam settlement.

shanty, and in the night there was a big fall of snow which lay on the tree, and as the tree went down the shanty went up. They went to work and cut it down, and all was right again....

Jonathan Crisp, seen here with wife Sarah and their children at their home in Fairholme, was one of the first settlers in Hagerman Township and a major force in shaping the community. The pioneer home Jonathan built is undoubtedly the only one on the Great North Road to have been continuously occupied by the original family into the 21st century.

Courtesy of Devina Crisp

The next step was to erect a more substantial home meeting the requirements of the Free Grants and Homestead Act. Because few homesteaders had the means to exceed the minimum dimensions required by law, Free Grant houses tended to be cast in the same mold: a simple box affair measuring 16x20 feet, constructed of hewn logs. There were two or three rooms downstairs, one of them a bedroom for the parents, and a steep set of stairs led to a low-ceilinged loft where children slept. Their sameness also reflected the fact that they were erected by the assembled menfolk of the community following a simple plan, the same one used in all the preceding bees. The process went like this: the newcomer felled a couple of dozen medium-sized, clean-trunked trees, usually white pine, on his lot, skidded them out to his clearing, and called a bee. Everyone within reasonable travelling distance, menfolk and womenfolk, felt an obligation to come because they had been similarly helped when they held *their* bee. The logs were chopped to length and hewn on two sides to a thickness of about eight inches, then dovetailed on both ends to interlock at the corners. Then, everyone pitched in to raise the timbers into place, forming a crib with apertures for windows and a door or two. Ten or so pairs of steeply-pitched rafters made of peeled balsam poles were added, a lumber roof was applied, and shingles split from blocks of straight-grained pine or cedar finished the job — although much chinking and finishing of the structure remained to be done as time permitted. Sometimes, a coat of room-

The hewn-log homes of the pioneers were typically one-and-one-half storey, as is this Brownley house in McKellar Township. It boasted one unusual feature: plaster, probably made using limestone found on the property, laid over lathes split from straight-grained wood.

brightening whitewash was applied to the interior surfaces of the hewn timbers, and often, insulating layers of newsprint were added in the continuous battle against cold. Very rarely, interiors were plastered, using a mixture of sand and locally produced lime applied over hand-split lathes.

Yet another reason for the Free Grant home's simplicity was that, like the shanty it replaced, it was intended merely as a stopgap until still better quarters — a substantial frame house at least, or perhaps even a fine brick one — took its place. In time, most of the settlers who stayed on did graduate to frame homes (and turned the old ones to advantage as extra barns), but very few brick structures of any kind would ever grace the Great North Road. Mary Millin also left us a description of building their first real home, atop a hill overlooking Whitestone Lake:

How shingles were made. The froe and mallet are from the Bell-McEwen farm at Fairholme.

> As there was no lumber or shingles to be had nearer than Parry Sound, my father went to work and made some during the winter months. He and the boys cut from a nice clear pine, some blocks for shingles the usual length, and some three feet long for lumber. With a dog and hand sleigh they drew them home, then they were split the desired thickness by means of a froe and maul; and the shingles were dressed with a draw-knife, and the lumber with a hand plane. In the spring they cut the logs [for the walls] and dressed them on both sides with a broad axe, and with a yoke of oxen they drew them together on top of the hill [overlooking Whitestone Lake] …a few men gathered to erect the walls of the house. Then it was roofed and floored with the home-made lumber and shingles. The doors were made by joining two lengths of lumber in the middle, and by September we settled in our new home.

Pine shakes on the roof of a log barn at Shawanaga Lake.

In an interview tape-recorded in 1969, Ethel (Sands) North recalled her childhood home:

> I was born in Fairholme in a log house Father built. He came from Ireland when he was 16 years old, and lived near Chatham and was married there. There was word came there was land granted, and Father and Uncle Henry Wye and Uncle Oliver Simpson [came up and] and settled all in a row in the middle of the bush. Father left Mother in Parry Sound, right near Beatty's

mill, and he worked there to get lumber enough to put into his house. He started chopping enough trees down to make a land to build his house on, and he made a fairly good house — there was the big living room and a bedroom and pantry, and three bedrooms upstairs. When Father got the house up enough, Mother came up. He didn't even have a floor into it, just a mud floor with a little wee hole in it for a cellar. They got a stove in Parry Sound, a great big range [with] an open fireplace in the front; we used to open the door and watch the fire burn. And they had a box stove [in another] room, but it was cold; when the fires would go out things would freeze up.

Taken about 1970 while it was being dismantled for reassembly elsewhere, this picture of Robert Andrews's house reveals how peeled balsam poles were used to make the rafters. Other details include chinking made with locally burned lime.

The first-generation barn, which provided shelter for livestock and a storage place for harvested fodder, was likewise a carbon copy of all others up and down the road. A pair of square cribs constructed of round cedar logs, separated by a 12-foot-wide "thresh floor" through which a wagon or sleigh could be driven, were the building's foundation and core. A loft above these held hay, and sheaves of grain waiting to be pitched down and threshed with a flail. One or both of the cribs, after the cracks between the logs were chinked with split lengths of cedar to keep out the cold, served as stabling.

Timber frame "bank" barns, built into sloping ground so that wagons could access the thresh floor from the rear, and livestock the lower stables from the front, began appearing on the scene in the 1890s. Most were erected on stone foundations; an abundance of raw material lay close at hand in the stone piles that ringed every field, and rare was the community that didn't contain at least one Old Country stonemason. A second practitioner, the barn framer, employing only square and compass as precision instruments, fitted out the many massive hewn timbers making up the frame. The test of a framer's expertise was whether or not, when each beam was raised into place, the holes, pre-bored to accept the oak dowels that would fasten it to its neighbour, lined up perfectly. Around the turn of the century, hardly a summer passed without a barn raising somewhere in each community. Like the house bees of a generation earlier, they were social affairs not to be missed. By now, dancing was gaining acceptance in a region where, earlier, such frivolity was frowned upon. Many a newly laid thresh floor was christened by the shuffling feet of barn dancers.

In an era when building was done entirely with highly flammable wood and fire departments were non-existent, the fear of being "burned out" hung over the countryside like a dark cloud. Rarely did a year pass without at least one family in any given community losing house or barn to fire. Poorly made chimneys, flimsily arranged stovepipes, over-heated stoves, lightning, and, in barns, upset lanterns and the spontaneous combustion of damp hay, lurked like demons ever ready to pounce on the poor homesteader and rob him of all he had worked for.

Macil (Cooper) Moore experienced a house fire in 1921, when she five years old, and recalled the ordeal in a memoir written for her grandchildren three-quarters of a century later:

A vacant house surrounded by maple trees stood near the shore of Whitestone Lake. There were two bedrooms upstairs, a large living room and two bedrooms downstairs. A family had lived in this farmhouse at one time [but] unfortunately the father [William Craig] drowned and his wife and children moved to [Dunchurch] as it was not a place for a mother to raise a family by herself.

My father [Dick Cooper] had hired men to bring logs up the lake to the mill to be cut into lumber. Because this was going to take several weeks of work, this seemed like an ideal place to stay. Father moved our family across the lake by boat, for there wasn't a road to the house. Mother [Agnes (Dobson) Cooper]

Mary Ann Madigan, daughter of Mr. and Mrs. Thomas Dickie, in front of the Dickie home near Limestone Lake north of McKellar. The Dickies first home was a shanty built nearby. According to family lore, when the shanty was finished, Thomas handed his wife his last 50 cents and went off to work the winter in a lumber camp.

Courtesy of Grace Crisp

Barns on the Dave Wye farm (originally homesteaded by William Moore) near Dunchurch.

The newly raised framework of Bob Farley's barn on Farley Road, built in 1913. Standing left to right are "Texas Bob" Moore, Ernie Carlton, Chris Junck, who framed the barn, and Bob Farley.

was coming to cook and she soon had the house spotless.... I will never forget the wonderful aromas… homemade bread, raisin and apple pies along with spice cakes, cookies and other warm and pleasant smells. My sister and older brother attended school in… Dunchurch. The only transportation available was by boat and then they would walk the rest of the way.

One sunny afternoon in June, Mother let my younger brother [Newton, age three] and me play outside. There was an old cookstove in the yard [and] we were dancing and playing on top of this old stove when I noticed a flame on the roof of the house. "Fire!" I screamed as I ran into the kitchen where Mother was preparing supper. "Mama, do you know there is a fire on the top of our house!" She hurried outside to look.

"Oh dear!" Mother exclaimed. Running back into the house, she began carrying things out. Thinking that I was helping, I grabbed a pot and cookie pan and followed her outside. "Don't come into the house," Mother said. "Both you and your brother stay back by the cedar trees." Since there was no telephone service available, no help could be called.

Mother ran upstairs and gathered clothes and blankets, which she threw down the steps. Wrapping blankets around

Buffet lunch at the raising of Robert "Grievous Bob" Moore's frame barn near Dunchurch.

[a mandolin and a violin belonging to the workmen] she tossed them to safety as well. She then ran into the bedrooms downstairs and dragged the springs and mattresses outside, calling to us to stay where we were. When Mother tried to move the trunk that carried many of our valuables, it knocked the door shut. She was then locked inside the room; the latch had caught on a crooked nail and she was trapped.

"Mama, come out!" we were shrieking. Hearing our frantic cries, she was frightened that we would come looking for her. With fear giving her strength, she broke the latch with her shoulder.

My brother Bill was 12 years old at the time and was on his way home from school when he saw the smoke. He jumped into the boat and rowed home across the lake, leaving my sister Lily because she was some distance behind. When he got home, he tied the boat and came running up the path shouting, "Where is Mama?"

"In the house," we told him just as Mama came out with more items. "Don't go in, leave the trunk," she begged, but he rushed in hoping to save more. Mother followed him with an axe to break [the door] down, thus saving the trunk and a few more clothes. The fire was crackling, smoke was stinging our eyes, and the flames were shooting high into the sky.

This scene of a newly-built Free Grant home and its occoupants was captured in the 1870s by Parry Sound amateur photographer Duncan Macdonald.

Rufus Harris worked in lumber camps as a young man, then took up farming at Waubamik. About 1930 he sheathed the farmhouse in brick, making it stand out as one of only a half-dozen or so such structures ever to grace the Great North Road.

When [Macil's sister] Lily saw the smoke, she ran to the shore and found the boat gone. Luckily, a farmer and his son arrived at the same time, and Mr. Simpson asked her if she could help Gilbert bail the leaky boat while he rowed to the other shore. It was hard work but they made it safely and ran toward the burning house. The men that worked for Father had started for home and, noticing the smoke, sped up the lake with the boat full speed. They were too late to save any more furniture, as the house was now engulfed in flames…. My mother was a small woman and the men were amazed over the amount of things she had saved. I remember them placing a mattress on the ground for her to lie on. She was so exhausted and had injured her arm on the blocked door.

The stove in the house had been burned, so someone lit a fire in the old stove outside that we had been playing on such a short time ago [and], having saved some food, supper was cooked.

CHAPTER FIVE

Leading Men

TODAY, ASIDE FROM the town of Parry Sound, the Great North Road boasts but two communities having a sufficiently large population to rate as villages. These are McKellar, 25 kilometres into the interior, and Dunchurch, another 15 kilometres farther along. Except on annual agricultural fair days, it is unlikely today that either can truthfully claim to contain more than 100 or 200 souls. Commanda, at the road's northern terminus, in the early years served as a vital service and distribution centre, but its growth was arrested as communication patterns evolved. All three communities were conceived with great expectations and promoted by pioneering individuals whose energy and vision set them apart from the ordinary crowd.

THE ARMSTRONGS OF MCKELLAR

The brothers Samuel and John Armstrong, sons of Irish immigrants to Ontario's County of York, arrived in the district around 1867, when Parry Sound was still little more than an idea and they were barely out of their teens. In due course, the boys' parents and one or more siblings arrived to join them in their enterprises, further imprinting the Armstrong stamp on McKellar (or, as the budding village was known in its infancy, Armstrong's Rapids).

First, the brothers Armstrong started a livery stable in Parry Sound. Then, they landed a contract for work on the Great North Road. They had already staked out three homestead lots for themselves along the road not far north of Parry Sound (including land presently occupied by the still-operating Loch farm immediately north of Portage Creek), but on viewing the place where the route bridged the narrows between McKellar Lake and Lake Manitouwabing, they would have recognized the rapids as an energy source capable of forming the nucleus of a future community. The brothers laid claim to two or three hundred surrounding acres, and in addition to clearing a farm, engaged a surveyor to lay out a village site. They first harnessed the waterpower to operate a sawmill producing lumber, shingles and lathe, then, around 1875,

Samuel and John Armstrong's store and post office in McKellar in the 1870s.

Courtesy of Duncan Macdonald/Ontario Archives F1023 Acc12318, AO5449

John Armstrong's
residence in
McKellar.

Courtesy of John Rogers

a gristmill which eventually boasted two millstones, one for "gristing" flour and one for "chopping" coarser livestock feed. By 1880, a woolen mill where subscribing farmers could have wool from their sheep turned into yarn, blankets and cloth would join the industrial complex drawing power from the rapids. Just beyond the bridge, the Armstrongs erected a combined general store and post office, and a hotel (a temperance establishment, in keeping with their Methodist principles) to serve the stream of homesteaders who followed them up the Great North Road. By now, they had expanded their operations to include a smithy, and a shop manufacturing wagons, buckboards and sleighs. The latter enterprise capitalized on the fine white oaks — ideal for making wheels and runners — found growing in clay soil surrounding Lake Manitouwabing. Sleighs, both heavy models for the log-haul and lighter cadge sleighs, were much in demand by lumbermen and so were turned out in quantity. Perhaps peculiar to McKellar was the factory's two-wheeled, spring-equipped "Armstrong cart," evidently designed with the region's rocky and swampy roads in mind.

A logging chain bearing the SJA stamp of logging contractors S & J Armstrong, which for nearly a century lay buried beside the Magnetawan River.

However, in the 1870s, the main chance to prosper lay in doing business not with poor settlers but with the large lumber companies that by now had nailed down rights to harvest the region's store of virgin pine timber. The brothers' first venture into that field seems to have been in the winter of 1868–69, when they logged for the William Beatty Company near Moon River, south of Parry Sound. The following winter they contracted with the Dodge Lumber Company, whose sawmill was at Byng Inlet, to take out their season's cut of timber along the middle reaches of the Magnetawan River. This marked their debut as logging "jobbers." Operating under the title S & J Armstrong, they contracted to build and equip lumber camps with sleighs, horses and a variety of tools and equipment, and hire gangs of lumberjacks to fell and haul the timber to lake or river, there to await the spring log drive. The Armstrongs were the first to conduct log drives down many of the district's streams and rivers, and therefore were responsible for carrying out the necessary "improvements" — the brushing out of the banks of streams, the removal of generations of tree trunks fallen across them, and the building of dams and slides to store water and facilitate the floating of logs. Many of the existing concrete control dams in the Seguin River watershed, for example, are direct descendants of log structures installed long ago by S & J Armstrong. This activity led inevitably to disputes with settlers. In the spring of 1877, Frank Ferris, a British Royal Engineers pensioner, found the land surrounding his homestead shanty on Lorimer Lake "covered by water, a nursery for disease, toads and insects" due to flooding caused by a dam installed on Still Creek. He claimed damages amounting to $20 from the Armstrongs and the Guelph Lumber Company. The Armstrongs paid up, but not the lumber company. When flooding persisted, Ferris allegedly cut open the offending dam, and as a consequence was summoned to court. Sentenced to jail, the proud Imperial Army veteran refused to enter the cells, sleeping instead in the gaoler's residence and taking his meals in a Parry Sound restaurant. Ferris struck back by suing the Armstrongs and the Parry Sound Lumber Company, some of whose logs also came down that branch of the Seguin River. The court again found against Ferris, prompting Liberal pundit Duncan Macdonald to report as follows to John B. Miller, owner of the Parry Sound Lumber Company and Liberal MPP:

Homesteader Frank Ferris found his land covered in water, "a nursery for disease, toads and insects."

Courtesy of James Ferris

> *Old Lorimer Lake Ferris got left on his suit with the Armstrongs and it's laughable to see the faces of both parties. Sam Armstrong's phiz. widens across from ear to ear & Ferris's mug drops down over his chin and looks like as if his nose would require a martingale on it to keep it from getting in his mouth. Old Moffat, Sam Oldfield and a few more of the obstructionists [Tories] around McKellar are tuning their wind instruments a notch lower down.*

Ferris and the Armstrongs would continue to irritate one another until, suffering from a condition he attributed to "the miasmatic vapors arising from the drowned land around my house," Ferris left Lorimer Lake and Canada to live with a son in Zion City, Illinois, where he died in 1904.

The Armstrongs' lumbering activities ranged as far north as the French River, and spanned well over two decades, embracing the peak years of the white pine logging era. In 1880, the partnership was said to be worth $20,000, then a modest fortune. That fall, they put 150 men in the bush to fulfill

When S & J Armstrong built this logging dam near McKellar, it raised the water of Lorimer Lake, and the ire of homesteader Frank Ferris.

Courtesy of John Rogers

contracts with four different companies to harvest a total of 13 million board feet of timber — perhaps 150,000 sawlogs in all. Ever watchful for new opportunities, when it became apparent a railway was due to cross the upper Magnetawan River at Burks Falls, they seized yet another opportunity by establishing a sawmill there. Requiring an extra long and thick stick of timber to serve as a bed for the line shaft that drove the mill's machinery, they had one made of stout McKellar oak, and in winter dragged it north to the Magnetawan River with teams of horses.

While John busied himself with the farm and the business of the partnership, older brother Samuel distinguished himself in public life. He was instrumental in having McKellar Township incorporated as a municipality (in 1873) and became its first reeve, and together with John played a leading role in forming an agricultural society that remains alive and well in the 21st century. Samuel served as McKellar's justice of the peace, was later appointed sheriff of the District of Parry Sound, and served a term as district member of the Ontario legislature. To some, in fact, the part Samuel Armstrong and his cronies played in Parry Sound affairs amounted to the tail wagging the dog. In a letter written to a friend in 1911 giving all the current gossip "on the Deadhead Corner around the Bank of Ottawa," Duncan Macdonald quoted a citizen, Harry Jukes, marveling at the monopoly McKellar people seemed to have on government jobs. "The sheriff [comes] from McKellar, and the deputy ditto, the typewriter is a McKellarite, Manson the Gaoler, Gibson the Turnkey, Jones the Division Court Clerk, Little the Bailiff, all from McKellar."

The Armstrong story was not one of uninterrupted successes (in 1890, the firm S & J Armstrong weathered a period of insolvency), but as pioneers operating at the cutting edge of the lumbering industry and founders of the community of McKellar, the family figures prominently in the story of the Great North Road. Throughout the settlement years, they were the primary providers of off-farm employment within a considerable radius of McKellar. Oliver Sands, who arrived in Fairholme as a child, in 1875, put it in a nutshell: "Money was a pretty scarce rig them days, and S & J Armstrong pretty near kept the country going. Give [the settlers] work for a bag of flour."

GEORGE KELCEY OF DUNCHURCH

When George Kelcey, reputedly a direct descendant of Sir Francis Drake, and a painter and decorator by trade in his native England, arrived in Parry Sound with his mind set on owning land in the wilds of Canada, the frontier had been pushed north into Hagerman Township. Finding an unoccupied tract of level land fronting the Great North Road about nine kilometres beyond McKellar, he claimed his 200 acres and began the daunting task of creating a clearing in the forest and providing a home for his wife, Lucy, and their young family. Like many others who found themselves in the vanguard of settlement, the Kelceys supplemented their means by stocking a few essentials for resale to later migrants, and making their homestead a "stopping place" where travellers could

George Kelcey, a self-portrait.

obtain a meal and a bed and stabling for the night — a logical venture given their situation about a day's travel from Parry Sound. Assuming a leadership role in community affairs, Kelcey dedicated a precious acre of his clearing for use as a burying ground — today's Fairholme Cemetery — and joined with Jonathan Crisp, an equally civic-minded English settler across the road, to marshal the manpower and resources of the neighbourhood to erect Hagerman Township's first schoolhouse.

However, Kelcey quickly recognized that the future commercial hub of the township was not to be Fairholme (a name Kelcey may have given to his own "estate" before it was adopted to identify a surrounding cluster of homesteads), but the narrows separating the upper and lower bodies of Whitestone Lake, eight kilometres farther north. There, he located additional acreage encompassing considerable lake frontage, perhaps claiming it in the name of his wife, a widely used method of securing additional property without violating the letter of the Free Grants and Homestead Act. Kelcey's new location

In 1870, George Kelcey claimed a homestead at Fairholme, where for three or four years his home served also as a store and stopping place. These artifacts were unearthed a century later, when the site became a gravel pit.

embraced half of the future site of Dunchurch, initially called Newcombe but renamed by Kelcey after his wife's birthplace in England.

Kelcey undertook to play the same role in Dunchurch as the Armstrongs in McKellar. On the north side of the narrows he built a substantial frame home, which also housed a store and post office, and a barn and stables. On the opposite bank he helped establish a smithy and the village's first hotel, in joint efforts involving Samuel Calvert and John Burns respectively. The slight drop in elevation between the upper and lower bodies of Whitestone Lake (named for an outcropping of pure-white crystalline limestone at the narrows) was insufficient to supply the energy needed for a watermill, so in 1877 Kelcey brought in a steam engine and boiler, and installed a sawmill immediately south of the narrows to cut lumber for sale to settlers. Some of its product went into a meetinghouse, a substantial frame structure known as Kelcey Hall that, with the help of volunteers, he built atop a gentle slope facing the lake. The hall served as a community meeting house, an Anglican church, a theatre for plays and concerts, and the Hagerman Township municipal office before it and a surrounding grassy acre were acquired by the local Agricultural Society as agricultural hall and fairgrounds. According to an account in *Along Memory Lane with Hagerman People,* when the local branch of the Women's Institute was formed in 1914, "things began to happen to this Hall." This dedicated group, which has remained active through four generations, took it upon themselves to upgrade the furnishings, even installing a new hardwood floor when the original one of pine wore out under years of punishment from dancing feet. Kelcey Hall, periodically enlarged and remodelled, served the community for a century before being demolished to make way for Dunchurch's present community centre.

It was not poverty but a need for a healthier work environment for George, who suffered from the effects of lead poisoning contracted from his paints, which brought the Kelceys to Canada. In 1880, the capital they brought over, augmented by the prospering enterprise in Dunchurch, enabled them to send their two oldest children, a boy and a girl, back to England for three years of schooling. But in 1884, only 14 years after it began, the Kelcey success story abruptly ended. While he was operating his sawmill, a piece of wood thrown off the whirling saw penetrated his skull, killing the enterprising pioneer and founder of Dunchurch.

The George Kelcey home lies just beyond the bridge over Dunchurch Narrows.

Courtesy of Myrtle Bashford

Only marginally noted in the written record is Lucy Kelcey, George's wife. Born Lucy Ann Manning in Dunchurch, England, she raised six children, three of them born before the Kelceys emigrated. In addition to these, five more offspring died either at birth or in childhood. She continued to run the store for some time after her husband's untimely death, then moved on to Loring to live with her eldest son, Ed, who had opened a store there, and finally went to California, where she died in 1933 at the age of 92 years. Lucy Kelcey symbolizes the poorly documented half of the pioneering story, and consequently of this book: that of the women who toiled equally as hard as the men in their joint venture on the frontier, and too often had to endure more than their fair share of the hardships involved. The Balsam Road's Ben Harvey summed up the lot of the pioneer wife as only an Irishman could. When his own wife, Mary Emma, fell ill and was hospitalized, Ben suddenly had all her responsibilities about the house and barn thrust upon him, and after a few frustrating days he declared to his hired man, "A man only knows half the work his woman has to do, and a man can't do the half of that!"

Lt.-Col. James Arthurs, commanding officer of Parry Sound District's 162nd Battalion.

COL. JAMES ARTHURS, MP, OF COMMANDA

In 1884, 18-year-old, high school-educated James Arthurs of Hamilton, Ontario, headed for the frontier and set himself up in business as a general merchant in the fledgling village of Commanda, set in a deep valley where the Rosseau–Nipissing Road bridged Commanda Creek. Commanda was the northern terminus of the Great North Road (the two colonization roads merged immediately to the north of Commanda) and the commercial and transportation hub of the surrounding region during the early settlement years. Until the Northern Railway reached Trout Creek 20 kilometres to the east of Commanda, Arthurs, who kept a team of horses for the purpose, hauled his store supplies all the way from Rosseau, 100 kilometres to the south.

As transportation patterns evolved, Arthurs, now a family man (he married Elizabeth Gillespie in 1887), saw that the Toronto–North Bay railway corridor offered an ambitious entrepreneur greater opportunities

A general store opened in Commanda in 1885 by James Arthurs now houses a splendid little museum displaying artifacts of earlier times. Curator Roberta O'Quinn stands on the verandah.

than Commanda, so he opened a hardware business in the budding trackside community of Powassan. He entered the political arena, winning the Parry Sound seat in the House of Commons on the Conservative ticket in the federal election of 1908, a victory he would repeat six more times, the last being in the election of 1930.

At about the same time as he threw his hat in the political ring, Arthurs joined and soon took command of the Powassan company of the 23rd Northern

The pine plank floor of the Commanda Museum is riddled with marks left by the calked boots of river drivers who did business in James Arthurs's store.

Pioneers, a militia unit embracing Parry Sound and Muskoka Districts. Late in 1915, Ottawa chose him to raise and lead an infantry battalion, the 162nd, for overseas service in the Great War. This did not sit well with Duncan Macdonald, who, as district organizer for the Liberal party, was nursing an open sore dating from the defeat of his own candidate in 1908, and aggravated by the fall of the Laurier government three years later. Furthermore, Macdonald had two officer sons of his own, whom he likely believed were better qualified for the lofty colonel's post. When, in the spring of 1916, Col. Arthurs assembled his battalion for training in a tent camp set up in a sandy field beside Lake Bernard, Macdonald sourly noted in his diary entry for May 22, "Jim Arthurs' Pot and Frying Pan Brigade go to Sundridge...."

In late October 1916, Col. Arthurs embarked for England with his 800-odd woodsmen, townsmen and farmers turned warriors. There, the 162nd Battalion was broken up to reinforce other Canadian army units whose ranks had been depleted in that summer's Battle of the Somme. Although he did spend a short time in France, by the spring of 1917, Arthurs, with no battalion to command, was back sitting in the House of Commons. The Commanda storekeeper's career path reached a summit in 1935, two years before his death, when he was called to the Senate.

CHAPTER SIX

Getting Started

TEN YEARS AFTER the district was thrown open to settlement, all of the land to a considerable depth flanking the road as far north as Maple Island had been taken up. In Hagerman Township alone, nearly one hundred individuals had registered claims on close to 20,000 acres. The average claimant, to quote colonization road supervisor J.W. Bridgland speaking of Free Grant settlers in general, was "not rife in pecuniary means, hence time and laborious patience must supply the lack of money for at least a few years." The settler's first task, after providing shelter for self and family, was to dispose of the trees that stood like an occupying army astride the land he'd claimed. Thick-trunked and deeply rooted, the virgin forest of pine and hemlock, yellow birch, maple and oak must have been daunting even to the most stout-hearted, and enough to turn away many others in discouragement. First, a few acres were "brushed," a process in which the understorey of shrubs and saplings was cut out. Then came "chopping," the felling of large trees and cutting their trunks into manageable lengths, work that could be done in any season of the year, including winter. This was all done with axes. As Dan Campbell, a son of Waubamik pioneers, once explained, "The old-time saws had no drag teeth [to carry the sawdust out of the cut], and a man could chop easier than he could saw." So it is no wonder that, high on the government-issued list of essential equipment for the homesteader, was a grindstone for keeping his axe

Clearing new land on the North farm near Whitestone Lake. Smoke from burning brush piles nearly obscures the forest edge in the background.

Courtesy of Amos North

sharp. Migrants from southern Ontario were familiar enough with the axe, but many of those coming from the British Isles had first to learn how to use it. In 1874, an Englishman named Joseph Dale published a pamphlet after travelling the Muskoka Road, which warned of this situation (plus a host of other difficulties) facing prospective immigrants: "The emigrant…having never perhaps as yet used a backwoods-mans axe, will find it necessary to employ one or two axemen — Canadians, who have been used to this sort of thing all their lives…. The axemen of course have to be fed, and rare appetites they have…."

The final stage was to "log" the tract and dispose of the trees by burning. "They'd clear a piece of land," Ethel (Sands) North remembered from her childhood days, "and have a bee and log it up. They'd cut trees down, and the logging bee would be to gather those trees all up. All the neighbours who lived around would come to have a logging bee, then they'd have a burning, and while the burning was on, they'd have a big time over that."

Those who had them brought oxen or horses to drag the logs into heaps. Any long pieces remaining might be sectioned by placing burning brands of dry wood over them at intervals. Smaller logs were pulled around and over the biggest ones, branches and limbs were piled on top, and when all was finished and dry weather arrived, the piles were set alight. If a fallow fire escaped into the adjacent bush, well, it was due to be cut down in coming years anyway, and in the meantime, the burst of new growth rising in the fire's wake would provide pasture for cattle, and wild raspberries in abundance for the womenfolk to pick and preserve.

Now, all that remained was a blackened clearing studded with tree stumps, among which the settler planted his first crop. The stumps would gradually yield to a combination of decay and sporadic attempts to uproot or burn them. The turf-free bush soil, charged with a pent-up supply of nutrients, at first needed no plowing, and for three or four years yielded good crops. The first plantings of seed were simply hand-broadcast onto the loose soil and raked over with a

Bob Gibson (left) and neighbour Henry North, both sons of pioneers, ploughing on the Gibson farm between Dunchurch and Maple Island.

Courtesy of Norman Gibson

homemade harrow — which might simply be a limb-studded treetop — to cover it. The first yields of garden produce, roots, peas and oats, were promising. The turnip, according to reports, sometimes yielded crops amounting to as much as 500 bushels per acre, with individual specimens approaching 20 pounds in weight. This could be literally a lifesaver, for in addition to providing food for livestock, a roothouse full of turnips sometimes sustained a family through winter, as Ethel North said of her parents:

> *The first winter they didn't have any [livestock], didn't have*
> *hardly anything to eat, either. They just cleared a little bit of land*
> *and the next summer Father planted turnips around where he*
> *had cut the trees down, and they lived on turnips for the first*
> *couple of years.*

In fact, it would take several years for a homesteader to achieve a reasonable degree of self-sufficiency. In 1876, in the order of 5,000 barrels of flour came into the district through the port of Parry Sound, mainly for the use of settlers in the interior. On sandy and acidic soil, the rule rather than the exception along the Great North Road, the initial fruitfulness merely gave the settler false hope, for typically the nutrients were exhausted after a few years of cropping. The only recourse was to keep on clearing more land — but in rock-ribbed Parry Sound District, opportunities to do so were decidedly limited. Happily, this harsh reality

For the first 30 years, before horse-drawn reapers and binders entered the scene, grain was cut with a cradle, then raked into piles for binding by hand into sheaves.

Johnny Somerville, and his homestead (following page) at Whitestone.

Courtesy of Bunty Croswell

did not always deplete the settler's sense of humour. Thomas "T" Lundy remembered his father, who homesteaded between Fairholme and Dunchurch, explaining with tongue firmly in cheek how he and his neighbour managed to each harvest a crop the first summer. By pooling their efforts, they got an acre along their mutual boundary nicely cleaned up by the beginning of June. Then, after standing the clearing on edge and each planting his side, they succeeded in filling both their roothouses with a winter's worth of turnips.

When George Kelcey relocated to Dunchurch, he continued to farm his Fairholme property in addition to some heavier clay land near Whitestone Lake, actively experimenting to learn which crops were best suited to the district, and promoting it wherever and whenever he could. *The Guide Book & Atlas of Muskoka and Parry Sound Districts* notes that in 1878, a sample of Kelcey's fine Early Rose potatoes had been "sent by the government agent to the Paris Exhibition." In 1880, the Ontario government, evidently now entertaining doubts about the region's suitability for farming, appointed a commission to look into the state of agriculture in Parry Sound–Muskoka. A trio of investigators toured the districts interviewing prominent members of farming communities. George Kelcey's deposition, taken at McKellar on September 1 of that year, needs to be read in the light of the fact that he had a vested interest in continued migration into the district. Nevertheless, it provides a revealing glimpse of conditions met by the first wave of Great North Road settlers.

> New land can be cleared up and fenced with rails and logs for $13 an acre.... I have between 500 and 600 acres of land, of which a little over 100 acres are cleared. One third of the soil is light and

two-thirds clay; about 25 per cent of the land is rough and rocky.... I sometimes manage to raise good crops of fall wheat on new land, but it does not pay to raise it on old land, as there seems to be something lacking in the soil.... I think lime is the element which the soil requires.... Crystallized lime is common in the neighbourhood, and though I have not used it on the soil I noticed that a few heads which grew near the lime kiln were excellent.... Oats are always a good crop in our settlement. I had 60 bushels to the acre last year, on land where there were a good many stumps.... I always seed down my land [to grass and clover] with the first crop, and plough it up after it has been in grass about five years.... My yield of hay averages $1\frac{1}{4}$ tons to the acre.... I have been very successful in growing turnips.... Potatoes do well with me; two years ago this fall I took 53 potatoes to Parry Sound weighing 63 pounds. ...Last year I planted 24 bushels, from which I got 450 bushels. I keep a number of sheep and cattle, including a bull, which is about half bred.... The people do not encourage the introduction of thoroughbred bulls; they would sooner put their cows to some common little bull running the road than pay $1 for the services of a thoroughbred. There has not been much stock raising...and nobody has come in with a view of sending cattle to the outside, as the local market is better. The lumbermen take nearly everything we raise... the settlers have never been able to supply the market, so that the lumbermen have to send outside for some of their supplies.... In the winter I feed my stock upon hay and straw, giving some turnips to my milch cows, and they do well on this food if kept in comfortable buildings.... I think stock raising should be carried on to a considerable extent, as the bush pasture

is a great advantage in the summer. I have a half-bred Shorthorn cow which has been living in the bush since the snow disappeared, and now she is the fattest animal in the neighbourhood; she is now good beef…. I brought some capital into the country with me, and find that farming pays me now, though it did not at first.

George Kelcey may have been the first — but far from the last — Parry Sounder to protest being lumped in with, or cast in an inferior light to, uppity neighbour Muskoka. Before signing a transcript of his evidence, Kelcey penned a pointed addendum:

Benefiting from the toil of their parents, the second generation of farmers had a somewhat easier start in life. Bob Gibson, son of the enterprising Hugh, is seen here with wife Irene shortly after their marriage in 1918.

I saw the reports of your meetings in the papers which read as though we were in Muskoka. It mentioned Mr. John Armstrong, of Muskoka, which is not correct…. In not mentioning it as Parry Sound our district sustains a certain amount of injury; everyone who reads the reports and thinks of moving to the free grants, will go to Muskoka. Half of our farmers travelled over Muskoka first and would not settle in it, and now are successful farmers in Parry Sound.

Appearing before the same committee, John Armstrong echoed Kelcey's opinion that the district's best agricultural prospects lay with beef cattle: "I think that for stock raising the Parry Sound district will yet prove to be one of the best parts of Ontario, though little or nothing has yet been done in that direction…. The pasture is excellent and the water pure and abundant…." Curiously, both Kelcey and Armstrong seem to have already forgotten the winter of 1878 –79, when cattle and horses starved due to a near failure of the hay crop of the previous summer. The price of hay rocketed to $20 a ton, if it was available at all, and settlers turned cattle into the bush to subsist on browse. That spring, a report on the McKellar local scene carried by the *North Star* stated, "The number of living skeletons of the bovine and equine species, around here, is something appalling." (The paper's McKellar correspondent, though, may just have been seeing things with a jaundiced eye that day, for that observation was followed with, "But mankind seems, in spite of Sunday-schools, church, and the N.P. [a political party then in power] as fat and sleek and wicked as ever.") It is noteworthy that the Parry Sound District farms still operating in the 21st century are mainly producers of beef cattle, proving Kelcey and Armstrong right.

Said to be the first agricultural settlers in McKellar Township, Andrew Moore and James McKeown claimed some of its best land, a tract adjacent to McEwen Lake offering both fertile soil and a reliable water supply. This modern view takes in parts of both of their locations.

Another glimpse of homestead life at that time is contained in a letter written by Mary Tait, a daughter of a McKellar pioneer. She arrived with a re-migration of settlers from eastern Ontario that saw her family and several others come to Parry Sound District, and a close friend, Annie Johnston, go to Michigan. Here are excerpts from a letter Mary wrote to Annie a few years later, in 1885:

> *We are living in McKellar in the district of Parry Sound. We have a farm within one mile of McKellar village and we are getting along well. We have 4 cows and a yolk of oxen and two young beasts and 5 sheep and 4 pigs and a splendid lot of fowls geese turkies hens and ducks and plenty of everything…. This is not a very good farming country but poor people seems to get along in it just as well as any place. I know for the most of the people that's in this place came in poor and all seems to be doing very well….*

Mary then spoke of mutual friends or relations who were doing even better, notably James Manson of Manson Lake on the Balsam Road, who "has a large stalk of cattle and a fine team of horses he drives out in his duble buggie…." The land surrounding Manson Lake is fertile clay, and the move up from oxen to horses signalled success. To what degree Mary's glowing report was just putting a brave face on things is hard to say, but she hit the nail on the head when she added that the average settler, being poor to begin with, was hardly worse off in Parry Sound.

A PROUD DAY AT FAIRHOLME

Cockney-born Jonathan Crisp, one of Hagerman Township's very first settlers, also rose to prominence as part of a small but active clutch of community leaders whose vision, wisdom and zeal molded it into a functioning society. When he was not busy promoting the educational, religious and governmental interests of the community, Crisp managed to clear and put under cultivation a substantial acreage at Fairholme. In 1907, his son David began a 20-year stint as proprietor of the homestead, an interval that descendants would remember as being beset by bears intent on devouring the family's flock of sheep. Dave managed to kill one large bear with a set gun, but his second encounter with his nemesis was of the direct kind, and in it he suffered a mauling, while the bear escaped to raid again.

Dave Crisp died prematurely at age 54, of pneumonia, and it is said that in the delirium preceding death he was once more locked in mortal combat with the black raider of the Crisp sheep pasture. He lies buried in Fairholme Cemetery, almost directly across the Great North Road from his home, but his real epitaph is found not on his gravestone but proudly carved in the woodwork of a 1900-vintage Massey-Harris grain seeder. Dave's father would have sown the seed for his first several crops of grain and hay simply by throwing handfuls to the right and left as he advanced across a field, or, as a first step up the technological ladder, by broadcasting it from a factory made, crank-operated seeder slung by a strap from the shoulder. The close of the 19th century saw a technological breakthrough in raising crops. Fields were now sufficiently large and stump-free to accommodate factory-made, horse-drawn planting and harvesting equipment, and farmers who had managed to put a little money aside began ordering seeders, disk-harrows, hay mowers, and reaping machines from implement dealers making regular rounds of the countryside. The Massey-Harris seeder pictured here reflects one such revolutionary event on the Crisp farm. A century after it rolled out of the Toronto factory of the first family of Canadian farm implement manufacturing, the seeder's original paint remains bright and its woodwork perfectly sound. Obviously, it was never allowed to sit out in the weather, evidence of how highly valued the labour-saving implement was. Just imagine — the operator *rode* as he worked! To remove any doubt as to the identity of its master, the youthful Dave Crisp one day took out his jackknife, leaned forward from the comfortable spring-mounted iron seat, and carved the words "D. Crisp Engineer" in the hardwood lid of the grain box. Today, the seeder is in the care of farm-implement buff Nelson Ward at McKellar, just a dozen kilometres removed from where it performed its life's work. Still protected from the weather, Dave Crisp's declaration of authority remains as crisply clear as the day he carved it.

Horse-drawn planting and harvesting machines, when they could be afforded, eased the lot of the homesteader. When his father acquired this made-in-Toronto Massey-Harris seeder (at right), young Dave Crisp laid claim to its cast iron seat by carving "D. Crisp, Engineer" in the lid of its grain box (below).

DIARY OF A DISCOURAGED HOMESTEADER

No sooner had the land rush to Muskoka–Parry Sound started than newspapers and pamphlets published in both Canada and the British Isles began exposing the "cruelty of sending newly arrived Immigrants to worthless Free Grant Lands." The government countered as best it could, in one instance promising that, while some settlers were indeed abandoning what proved to be useless locations along colonization roads, a little diligent searching would turn up plenty of good soil "around the thousands of lakes and lakelets that nestle among the rounded mountain peaks and hills" of the Shield. But for those on the ground there was no arguing with the hard facts.

On May 7, 1879, five men from Ingersoll, Ontario — Jasper Gorham, William Hunt, Stephen Houghton, Frederic Williams and Percival Langford — outfitted themselves with a muzzle-loading shotgun, a hunting knife, two or three axes, some blankets, clothing, salt pork and bread stuffed in carpet bags, and headed north seeking land. By then, everything bordering the roads had been claimed, so they settled more or less blindly for a block of remotely situated lots lying north of the Magnetawan River and an hour's walk east of Maple Island, the nearest established settlement. Only one of the five, Jasper Gorham, would stay permanently in the north, and he settled a few kilometres to the west in Whitestone. Location claims were never filed on any of the lots the group selected, and they remain Crown land today. This happened numerous, mostly forgotten, times. But Percival Langford, age about 24, kept a diary during his abortive attempt at homesteading. The group stayed in an empty lumber camp while throwing up a shanty in the centre of the block of lots, then began making sporadic attempts at clearing land. Between times, they worked for settlers around Maple Island in exchange for labour, provisions or cash, sleeping under whatever roof was handy.

May 16: Started from the lumber shanties about 7 o'clock found Jasper's lot. Started putting up a shanty…. Jasper & I fitted the logs we got on pretty well for greenhorns…

May 17: Started from the Lumber Shanties early for Jasper's lots went to work on the shantie Stephe and Fred cut cedar troughs for the roof Jasper and I built up the logs and put on some troughs. We started for the Lumber Shanties about 5 o'clock & cut a road through the woods pretty good nights rest.

[A number of pages of the diary are missing]

June 6: We slept 5 in a bed last night went to work on the road in the morning we worked till about 3 o'clock then went to Atkinsons to grind 2 axes we went over to H [Hugh] Gibsons for pork got 19 pounds I paid for the Flour pork & tea it come to $5.55 Stephe & Fred went back to Atkinsons I slept at Gibsons at night….

June 8: …fell in with [an] Englishman an Army Pensioner [named Powling] had a great talk about home he is going to take land up by us went back to Atkinsons. Slept in the barn it rained very hard all night.

June 9: …We started for the woods in the morning with Pattersons to work for them ¹/₂ day and all come back to the Shantie Slept on the ground the mosquitos were very bad we had a very poor nights rest Sung Songs till late at night.

June 10: Went to chop for Pattersons in the morning Fred and I went to find my [lot] it rained hard all afternoon we got drenched to the skin got back to the shantie took of our clothes wrung them out & dryed them by the Fire. The Dixons came there at night I slept on the ground under the bed.

June 11: Baked our cakes in the morning then started for Father's Lot [evidently Percival had claimed a lot for his father] we found the centre stake about Noon Fred & I chopped on his till 5…

June 12: After getting the cooking done Fred & I started for his Lot we got there about 11 o'clock went to work under brushing till 5 o'clock then Started for Dixon's shantie…Started smudges to drive away mosquitoes Dixon come back with the Oxen & stayed there all night…

June 13: Fred & I went to my lots in the morning Started chopping and under brushing at the Centre Stake We got along pretty well the flies were not very bad we set fire to some old [Birch?] the first time I have felt good we have had fried cakes for Supper

Maple syrup-making was a family affair. These women are "boiling down" near Dunchurch.

Courtesy of Muriel Macfie

Immence improvement on the old Style of cake. Slept pretty well in our clothes.

June 14: *Helped Mr. Dixon log till 4 o'clock then started for Mr. Atkinsons I went over to Luis French and got Stephes Boots we had supper at Mr. Atkinsons we slept in the house had all our clothes off slept splendid Stephe & Fred was going to start Tomorrow for Ingersoll.*

June 15: *…Fred & Stephe started for home…. I went over to Crawfords had dinner there…. Uncle [William Hunt] came over he had been working at Mr. Parkers Mr. Crawford came home from the [Byng] Inlet. I stayed at Crawfords at night….*

June 16: *Planting Potatoes for Louis French…. I went over to Mr. Parkers to see Uncle about going to the Inlet with Mr. Crawford he… went with him about 4 o'clock in the Canoe Down the River I…made an axe handle for Luis French & slept there at night.*

June 19: *I went to John Parker's to help him build fence we split 180 rails & laid up 357 he paid me 75 [cents] for the day I bought*

To collect maple sap, the homesteader simply chopped a diagonal notch in the trunk of a maple, and wedged a cedar slab into the lower end of it to direct a trickle of fluid into a wooden trough. No thought was given to harming the tree, which was likely to be felled in future land clearing anyway. Thomas Inwood tapped this maple near Dunchurch around 1880, then surrendered his tiny clearing to the surrounding forest. Over a century later, the tapping scar remains clearly evident.

25 cts of Pork from him & started at $^1/_2$ past 8 for Crawfords I slept there at night Saw a porcupine in the road going to his place

June 20: Started 7:30 for Dixons Shanty got there at 9 o'clock they were planting Potatoes I shouldered my axe and made for Fathers lot I underbrushed till 4 o'clock then started back for the Shanty there were fresh tracks of a Bear on the road to our Lots there was two River Drivers at the shantie

June 22 [Sunday]: Went in the morning with Luis and J Atkinson over in the canoe to get some Flour…in the afternoon had a nice walk home to Crawfords…. I spent the day pretty dull and lonely

June 23: Started for McKellar at 6 o'clock got there at noon went to Armstrongs for work they did not want anyone so I started back home at 3 o clock I saw a deer on the way had tea at Mr. [Jonathan] Crisps past the Village of Fairholme a very nice place got as far as Dixons Stopped there all night

June 24: Started from Dixons in the morning got to Atkinsons had Dinner saw Uncle he had come back the day before him & Crawford went over the Rapids & [Mr. Crawford] was Drowned & Uncle was saved I went and Engaged with Mr. Mortimer for $13 per month.

William Hunt had set out with Mr. Crawford of Maple Island to paddle 50 kilometres down the Magnetawan to Byng Inlet, hoping to find employment in a sawmill. Accounts conflict as to whether the accident happened on the way downriver, or on the way back after the two failed to find work. When the canoe was swamped, Hunt managed to crawl onto a rock in midstream, where he stayed until rescued a day or two later by passing river drivers, but Crawford was swept downstream and drowned. On June 26, word reached his widow and two small children in Maple Island that his body had been recovered and buried by the riverside. Percival Langford worked around Maple Island for a few more weeks, then paid his little clearing in the bush one final visit:

> August 4: *Went with Mr. Powling to hunt over my Land we tried to burn the Fallows but they would not burn…my gun went off accidentally sent the charge through my coat collar.*

> August 5: *Slept at Mr. Mortimers last night he sent me to help Luis French Log while he went to borrow money to pay me with…*

> August 6: *…went down to the Magnetawan had a Bathe then…stayed with Jim Lawrence till four o'clock when we Started for McKellar we walked all night got to McKellar 3 o'clock had Breakfast at the Thompson House*

> August 7: *Started for Parry Sound at 9 o'clock fell in with another man going there very rough all the way feet were very sore got there 5 o'clock…we stopped at Dukes Hotel slept very sound…*

In early times, maple sugar was cheaper than the imported kind, so every homestead had its sugarbush where the sap was boiled down into syrup or sugar in large kettles. This picture was taken in the mid-20th century, but the sugarbush was first tapped 75 years earlier by a homesteader named Calvert, who in his first year tapped about 30 maples and made six or seven gallons of syrup, making a cash crop of some of it by selling a gallon or two to the Dunchurch Hotel.

Early in the 20th century, Langton Carr of Commanda installed a large sap evaporator in a hewn-log building, tapped over two thousand maples, and produced hundreds of gallons of maple syrup each spring. This picture, taken in the sugar camp in 1913, includes most of the 13 children raised by the Carrs.

Courtesy of
Charles B. Milbank

August 8: *Started for Collingwood at 6 a.m. Breakfast on Board the Magnetawan the wind blew a strong gale all the way got to Collingwood 1 p.m. Got on board the cars for Hamilton at 3.10 ticket $2.85 took the cars at Hamilton for Ingersoll at 12.50 got home 2.50 a.m.*

Percival Langford became a successful dairy farmer at Ingersoll, and never returned to Maple Island. Ninety years after he left, in 1969, his son Albert came north, retracing his father's steps, and at that time allowed me to copy parts of his father's diary.

Others were even quicker to turn their backs not just on Parry Sound but on Canada, as was noted in a sketch of Dunchurch compiled in 1946 by a Mr. Pelletier, who occupied the position of schoolteacher there that year: "[About 1880] a group of Scottish settlers arrived, consisting of eight families. Of this group James Clelland, John Rae, Robert Rae and John Campbell stayed, while the other four families remained only a week and returned to Scotland."

Chapter Seven

Hotels and Stopping Places

TRAVEL, TEDIOUSLY SLOW in the days of oxen, quickened somewhat when horses took over. (Among the first men north of McKellar to acquire a team of horses was Cockney-born Jonathan Crisp, a fact preserved in history by the story that when he was attempting to overtake a jumper pulled by a plodding pair of cattle, he impatiently shouted to the driver, "Get those hoxen hoff the road!") Still, a fair day's journey given the usually bad state of the Great North Road, amounted to but 30 or 40 kilometres, so establishments offering food and shelter for man and beast were required at frequent intervals. Some of these, usually run as a sideline by settlers or small storekeepers, were known simply as "stopping places," while others were substantial enough to rate the name "hotel." The latter were of two kinds, those licensed to sell liquor, and "dry" establishments, generally referred to as "temperance hotels." The Temperance movement, vigorously promoted by influential figures such as Parry Sound's William Beatty and McKellar's Armstrongs, and subscribed to by a devout class of Protestants who made up a fair share of the settlers, was a big issue of the day. Dunchurch pioneer and strict Methodist Arthur Millin opened a temperance establishment in that village to run in opposition to a liquor hotel just down the street. As if to underline the dryness of the place, the village well stood squarely in front of Millin's establishment and the village jail perched atop a hill immediately behind it.

However, the wants of a thirsty transient traffic, particularly that generated by lumbering, had to be met. The *Parry Sound North Star,* fiercely temperance in its outlook, editorialized in its August 8, 1879, issue, "It is said the Nipissing and Parry Sound Roads from Bracebridge to Nipissing contain a beer agent to every three miles." The Great North Road was hardly less well appointed with watering places. Licensed hotels were a magnet for lumberjacks turned loose during the hiatus between the

The many-roomed Thomson House, situated a stone's throw from the point of commencement of the Great North Road, had been renamed the Kipling by the time this photograph was taken, around 1910.

Courtesy of H. Clare

HOTEL KIPLING, PARRY SOUND, ONT.

end of the cutting and hauling season and the start of the river drive, and again between the arrival of the sawlogs at Georgian Bay and the reopening of the camps in the fall. Parry Sound's nickname, "Parry Hoot," originated as the rallying cry of river drivers who, after drawing their pay at the end of the Seguin drive, headed for Parry Harbour and its hotels. Rivalry prevailed between different drive gangs and between men hailing from different communities. The cry "Whoop McKellar!" coming from the lubricated throat of a man from that quarter could ignite a free-for-all in a room full of loggers. It is said that a perennial feud, or more likely just a rowdy rivalry, which existed between the Campbells of Waubamik and the Macklaims of Hurdville, often boiled over into roughhousing when members of those clans found themselves sharing a barroom.

The nearest liquor hotel to the jumping-off point of the Great North Road was the Thomson House, a hundred yards distant on aptly named Champaigne Street. Three-and-one-half storeys high and advertised as capable of housing 250 guests, it served the travelling and drinking public for 35 years before burning down on Saturday night, March 27, 1915. At this, Duncan Macdonald, faithful recorder of the local scene and himself not above taking an occasional stroll across the bridge for a glass with a friend, was moved to remark, "A big hot Scotch in the Harbour last night after the legal license hours...by half past 9 o'clock the Kipling [as it had been renamed] was a pile of broken brick, crumbled plaster, ashes, and smoke." This he followed with the lament, "The palmy days of booze [are] about done...in Parry Sound." Riding a

Built in the 1870s by Henry Watkins but soon acquired by Parry Sound hotelier W.F. Thomson, the McKellar House advertised itself as "situated in one of the most picturesque villages in the Free Grant District of Parry Sound."

Courtesy of John Moffat

wave of wartime patriotic zeal, the old bugbear, Prohibition, loomed only months in the future. Unlike other liquor hotels that suddenly went up in flames about that time, the Kipling was rebuilt and, except during the Prohibition years, carried on as Parry Sound's main drinking place until burning down again late in the 20th century, this time to stay.

Gerald Markham, who arrived in Dunchurch with his parents as a child of six in 1887, and late in his life compiled a brief memoir of early times, pictured the local hotel scene as follows:

> On Saturday night, after a hard week on the farm or in the bush, some of the men met at the village hotel and got gloriously drunk together, with occasional rough-and-tumble fights, but the contestants settled their disputes themselves and whatever the outcome, seemed to remain good friends. About 1890, a log gaol

was built on the hill back of the village, but I don't remember anyone ever being put in it. The village was a crime-free community. Men seldom drank alone. They invited everyone to belly-up to the bar and have a drink. A quart bottle of whisky cost $1.00 and each drink 5 cents. It was taken neat. Partly because I was young and couldn't afford it, I did not drink, and was depended on to see that everyone in my party got home safely. Left on their own, their horses would always find their way home, but I remember one bitterly cold night when a man was left on a sleigh all night. His feet were badly frozen and resulted in the loss of several toes.

Northbound travellers arriving at Loring could find food and lodging at Kyle's stopping place, or if they stayed with the main road all the way to Commanda, at Evers's substantial premises in the village itself, or at Langton Carr's large farmhouse just short of where the Great North Road merged with the Rosseau–Nipissing Road. Charles B. Milbank, a grandson of Langton Carr, remembers his mother telling this story:

When the 13-bed Armstrong House, directly across the river from S & J Armstrong's milling complex in McKellar, was leased in 1893 by David Patterson to W.J. Jones, the agreement included a condition forbidding the use of intoxicants on the premises.

Courtesy of John Moffat

Langton Carr's prosperous homestead, just west of Commanda, marked the final mile of the Great North Road and served as a stopping place for travellers. Here Carr is seen standing, with his democrat and fine team of drivers, on the road in front of his home.

Arthur McDonald's hotel in Ahmic Harbour in 1903, with the *Wenonah* at the steamer dock. The spacious establishment, clad in bright red brick manufactured nearby in John Croswell's brickyard, was destroyed by fire not many years after this picture was taken.

Courtesy of Willis Kenney

Artifacts dug from the site of the Cataract House. The large broad axe (the handle was added later) is from the early logging days, when the finest white pine trees were made into square timber for the British market. The second largest object is a smoothing iron, which seems out of place so far in the bush.

The stage used to stop there overnight, and one of the stage drivers used to sneak out to the barn at two or three a.m. and steal oats from the granary for his horses. Grandpa knew what was going on and set a trap at the turn button to the granary door, where he had to reach around a corner in the dark. It wouldn't be an animal trap, I guess, but something that would hold onto his arm. In the morning when Grandpa was going to do the chores, he saw the man caught in the trap. As he passed him, he said, "When I get through the milking, I'll let you loose."

Several hours before reaching Loring or Commanda, a traveller would have passed, and likely stopped for refreshment at, the Cataract House, situated at the crossing of the Ferrie River. This general vicinity was for some time known as Glenila, after the nearby post office of that name. Established by Robert "Roarin' Bob" Montgomery, the Cataract House soon became colloquially known as "The Wildcat" as a result of the notoriety it gained during the 25 years it operated before being destroyed by fire early in the 20th century. Positioned on the frontier of a large tract of wilderness broken only by a scattering of logging camps, it did a booming trade with lumberjacks. Speaking of area hotels in general, on coming out of the bush for a spree a man sometimes would hand the hotel-keeper all his money at the outset, and when his bar, lodging and meal bill reached that amount, he was so informed, and he packed his turkey and took the cadgeroad back to camp. Roarin' Bob earned legendary status for the direct approach he took in handling unruly customers — with his fists. No doubt egged on by the sober-sided majority of settlers, the authorities closely scrutinized the activities of liquor hotels, and their licenses were subject to annual review, a time of concern for the hoteliers. Writing on April 20, 1892, Duncan Macdonald remarked, "License commissioners met today in the Court House and the country tavern keepers were in town in droves." Three years later, Montgomery's renewal application was refused by the commission, but apparently he got the ruling overturned, for the Cataract continued to operate into the new century, putting an enduring stamp of notoriety on a geographical reference point that, a hundred years after the hotel itself burned down, continues to be referred to as The Wildcat. As a child, Pearl [Buchanan] MacLennan would pass through that section during annual expeditions by buggy with her parents to visit her grandmother who lived several miles further up the road, and here is how Pearl remembered those trips: "After you crossed the second bridge in Maple Island they called it 'Little Hell,' it was so wild up there. Booze and bush and the Wildcat Hotel and wildcats and shantymen, all mixed up...."

James McAvoy was one rural hotelier who clearly succeeded in his profession. A native of Barrie, Ontario, he was advised by his doctor at the age of 20 to go north for his health. He first found work as a handyman around the Dunchurch Hotel (one chore he particularly remembered was feeding the six stoves it took to heat the place). In a few years, he saved the $1,000 it took to buy a hotel farther up the road at Whitestone, whose owner, named Hanlon, had decided to join the exodus to the West. After the first wave of lumbermen had creamed off the best pine, the area was now in a slump, and McAvoy could not be sure the Whitestone Hotel was a bargain even at its fire-sale price. But the tide abruptly turned when two wagons carrying some American lumbermen pulled up.

Pictured here in 1903, the Dunchurch Hotel, built by John Burns and run by a succession of hoteliers, burned down about the time of the Great War and not long before Prohibition was enacted. In its heyday it boasted "first class wines, liquors and cigars, good stables and an attentive hostler," as well as daily stage connections with steamers at Ahmic Harbour, and access to "the best hunting and fishing grounds." Behind the white horse is the village smithy, built by village founder George Kelcey and first operated by Samuel Calvert.

Courtesy of Willis Kenney

McAmmond's stopping place and post office at Glenila.

Courtesy of Esther Einarson

They had come to look over a "logged out" timber limit embodying several surrounding townships, with a view to buying it and utilizing a vast store of lower-grade timber that remained standing. A deal was closed and a new era of prosperity dawned. One memorable night, McAvoy crammed nearly a hundred paying guests, mostly wayfaring lumberjacks, into every available nook and cranny. Before the bloom wore off the logging boom, sportsmen discovered the great fishing and hunting to be had on the Whitestone frontier, adding a shot in the arm to the hotel trade. Soon, McAvoy was well enough fixed to move up in the business by selling out at Whitestone and taking over operation of another faltering hotel, the Mansion House at the corner of James and Mary streets in Parry Sound. At that moment, Parry Sound was on the threshold of a boom brought about by an Ontario government ban on the export of raw sawlogs to the United States, which dumped fresh business into the laps of three big sawmills on the town's waterfront. Fifteen years later, McAvoy, still not 50, sold out. He retired in Parry Sound and lived well into his 90s, so his doctor's advice, back in 1889, proved to have been wise.

CHAPTER EIGHT

Schools, Meeting Houses, Churches

THE FREE GRANTS settlers — a cross-section sample of society of the Victorian era — were by and large God-fearing and determined that their children should have both an education and a religious upbringing. So, as soon as a cluster of homesteads began to jell into a community, some citizen usually stepped forward to donate an acre of land as the site for what would serve as its cultural hub — a combined school, church and meetinghouse. In a way it was a self-serving gesture, in that it meant his own children would not have far to walk to school and Sunday school, but it can be no coincidence that in most cases those same people played a leading role in community affairs in general.

Hugh King, who arrived in the vanguard of Hagerman Township settlers, donated land for the Fairholme schoolhouse. Neighbours Jonathan Crisp and Henry Wye hewed the pine logs for its construction, a bee was called to throw up the walls and roof, then Crisp applied the finishing touches while Wye hammered together the pine benches that served as furnishings.

A count made in 1879 of school-houses in Parry Sound District (including the parts served by the Nipissing, the Parry Sound, and the Great North colonization roads) revealed a total of 23, eight of which were of frame construction and the rest of log. During the next three years, as immigration continued and the offspring of the early comers grew older, the number nearly doubled, to 44 schools. Those 23 schools of 1879 registered an enrollment totaling 890 pupils, but average attendance, as noted by J.B. MacDougall in his book *Building the North,* was less than half that figure: 369, or 16 pupils per school. Writing in 1877 about the scattered settlements of the Precambrian Shield, J.B. Hodgins, Deputy Minister of Education, iden-

By 1875, the community of Waubamik (Ojibway for "white beaver") boasted enough children to warrant a school, and in that year local sawmill owner Paul Leushner canvassed his neighbours and drummed up the necessary support. The resulting schoolhouse was built of lumber cut by Leushner, rather than the usual hewn timbers.

Courtesy of Hubert Harris

This large group of Waubamik schoolchildren (and a few adults) was photographed in the 1890s. By two decades later, the student body had shrunk considerably.

Courtesy of Hubert Harris

tified the main cause of the shortfall: "One of the great difficulties to overcome is bringing the schools within reasonable distance of the children of settlers in the backwoods. [We] see no means by which miles can be shortened, or natural barriers such as swamps, rivers, lakes and rocks removed."

In 1882, School Inspector Peter McLean remarked on a second problem specific to Parry Sound District, where "eight schools were closed through utter inability to pay teachers for longer than three months of the year." Furthermore, these were uncertified teachers "because they cost less." The provincial contribution toward operating 44 schools that year totaled only $426, under $10 per school. McLean also emphasized the problem of access, noting that some children lived too far from a school to go at all, while others were walking three or four miles over roads that "are long, continuous bog holes."

About 1940, an effort to record the histories of district schools was launched by Inspector of Public Schools J.L. Moore and continued by Peter Scott, who succeeded Moore in 1942. Teachers were told to compile narratives of their schools, drawing on such documents as existed and information supplied by older citizens. Following are excerpts from the submission of William Smith, teacher at the Maple Island school in 1944:

> As the community in Ferrie and McKenzie Townships expanded,
> a school became necessary. A petition dated March 30th 1883
> was presented to Mr. Peter McLean, Inspector of Public Schools
> for Parry Sound District [but based at Milton, Ontario], by the

following petitioners: Charles Mortimer, Edward Cannell, William McAmmond, John A. Parker, Mathew Gibson, Justice LaBrash, William Shaw, and John Brear....The petition was granted and the formation papers were drawn up and signed by Patrick McCurry, the judge for the District of Parry Sound, and Peter McLean...on April 18, 1883. The original school was built on lot 35, Concession 4 of McKenzie Township. John LaBrash donated the site. The building was constructed of hewn hemlock logs, size 12 by 24 feet. As the school was built in the woods on the hillside, no provision was made for a fenced in playground. The students were allowed to run in the woods.

The [teacher's] furnishings were very scanty, consisting of a home made table, fitted with a drawer. Handmade desks and benches were used by the students. Three twelve-inch boards painted black, nailed together when green, served as blackboards. These shrank when they became dry and left cracks wide enough to serve as a ledge for a pencil. A large square box stove in the centre of the room supplied the heat.

The students who first attended the school ranged in ages up to 24 years. Some of them, I am told, were young men with full-grown beards. [That year] was known as the year of hard times, [and] there was scarcely any work, [and] for this reason all the young men came to school. This school was burned in or about March, 1891 [then] the present school was built on lot 35, concession 3, Ferrie Township. It is a frame structure, size 18 by 24 feet... the library now consists of 349 volumes valued at $134.91. In 1937 the school was painted inside, and a new hardwood floor

Dunchurch schoolboys smile for the camera and roughhouse in the schoolyard about 1928 (top & middle). Pupils of the same school in a dress rehearsal for the Christmas concert of 1928 (above).

Courtesy of Gordon Powell

The Maple Island schoolhouse where the young Gordon Powell taught for three months in 1925.

Courtesy of Gordon Powell

was added. Lightning rods were placed on the building. Pictures were donated by the Imperial Order of the Daughters of the Empire. A new stove was added in 1941 and new slate blackboards in 1943.

The region's rural school boards had difficulty retaining teachers for any length of time — when they could lure them into the bush at all. It is a telling fact that no fewer than 50 individuals had held the Maple Island teaching post prior to William Smith, an interval spanning only 60 years.

Following the Second World War, the Department of Education launched a sweeping program of rural school consolidation, spearheaded by public meetings convened by the district inspector of public schools. After attending one held in Dunchurch in 1962, local pundit W.T. "Dub" Lundy described how the inspector filled a blackboard with masses of figures purporting to demonstrate that a central facility could replace half a dozen one-roomed schoolhouses scattered from Fairholme to Ardbeg, without it costing taxpayers one extra cent, then gave the baffled assembly half an hour to discuss the concept among themselves. "Of course," Dub wryly observed, "in a few minutes everybody was selling cows." The move faced considerable opposition, based in no small part on the argument that closing local schools would eliminate the centres of gravity that held long-established communities together, but in the end government coercion prevailed. A multi-roomed Whitestone Lake Public School was built in Dunchurch, while a flock of one-roomed schoolhouses in the outlying area were relegated to history.

Gordon Powell beside his Model T Ford.

Late in life, Powell appended these words to this picture of himself and Jessie Simpson:

When love was of today, and not a burden for the years,

A fleeting glimpse of sunshine caught from out the clouds of tears,

And neither was a kiss a cord to tie youth to a stay,

But just a coin from Pleasure's hoard, both won and spent today.

Courtesy of Gordon Powell

A SCHOOLTEACHER IN LOVE

The Great North Road of today is richly infused with pedagogical genes, for the majority of the rural schoolteachers who were attracted to the district in its first 75 years were young women who often as not were quickly wooed and won by local swains and absorbed invisibly into the community, leaving their vacated schoolhouses to be occupied by yet more young women from "outside." Male teachers, on the other hand, tended to be always remembered as such (who said life is fair?). A good example is Gordon Powell of London, Ontario, who, in 1924, when barely out of his teens, accepted a temporary teaching job at Maple Island. This foot-in-the-door posting led the following year to an appointment to the larger Dunchurch school, and during his 14-year tenure there, his name became firmly fixed in local history.

Riding herd on 40 pupils spread over 10 grades and crammed into the single room of a former Methodist church, Powell quickly made his mark, both on the strapped palms of recalcitrant schoolboys and in the community's eyes as a capable and respected shaper of its youth. And yet, when school let out, he did not hesitate to let down his fashionably slicked-back head of hair.

Powell added the following nostalgic footnote to this 1929 scene of himself at the wheel of his Whippet roadster, with Jessie Simpson at his side:

My Shangri-La — I had found it, but I hadn't the sense to grip it:

And I lost the prettiest girl in town, and I sold the little green Whippet!

Courtesy of Gordon Powell

Powell's extra-curricular interests consisted of his big dog, Pedro, sporty cars, and the current crop of Dunchurch's eligible young women. For the author of this book, mere mention of the name, "Gordon Powell," always invokes an image of a green Whippet roadster speeding past our front gate with Pedro planted firmly on a front fender and a local belle riding at Powell's side. Powell kept a photograph album during his Dunchurch years, then,

The highlight of the year in any rural school was the annual Christmas concert, attended by the entire community. This painting is of Sunny Slope school about 1930.

some 40 years later, added commentary to the pictures, mostly in verse form. The collection, recently donated by Powell's son, Michael, to the Whitestone Historical Society, affords a rare peek into the out-of-school life of a young male rural schoolteacher.

Powell's first car was a Model T Ford, and his first Dunchurch girlfriend was Mary, the fair-haired daughter of his landlady, the widow Mrs. Tom Buchanan, owner of one of the village's two general stores. The album also hints at one or two other brief romantic interests, but the supreme love of Powell's early Dunchurch years clearly was the vivacious Jessie Simpson (whom he unaccountably nick-named "Spaghetti"), only daughter of local lumberman and carpenter Thomas Simpson. By this time, Powell had traded up to the racy Whippet, and as previously mentioned, the combination made a lasting impression on the mind of a

In 1896 Dunchurch's Scottish element banded together to erect a Presbyterian church, sheathing their handsome creation in Ahmic Harbour brick. Today it is a charge of the United Church of Canada.

small boy weeding in our roadside garden. As it happened, when Gordon Powell finally did marry, in 1937, it was to Edna LaBrash of Maple Island, a daughter of the household where he boarded during the few months he taught there. Jessie Simpson herself took up the teaching profession, accepted a position at Orrville, east of Parry Sound, and true to form soon married a local farmer, Harvey Wilson. However, this turn of events in no way dilutes the romantic flavour of those pages of Gordon Powell's snapshot album.

Maple Island's church and cemetery, photographed in 1967.

◄◦►

Religion, like so much else, ascended the Great North Road bearing the stamp of William Beatty, staunch Wesleyan Methodist. After furnishing Parry Sound with a church building, inaugurating camp meetings for the Natives of nearby Parry Island, and launching his town on a temperance path, Beatty turned his attention to the budding settlements of the interior. The report of the Methodist Missionary Society for 1872–73 reveals that a mission and place of worship were now functioning in McKellar, and that "We have a church in the course of erection at Whitestone Lake." This "church," the first in Dunchurch, was in truth a combined school, meeting house, and centre of worship erected on land donated by pioneer settler Arthur Millin. Many years later, Millin's daughter Mary would explain:

> People began to talk about Church and School, for there were quite a number of children in the settlement by this time. So a meeting was called to talk the matter over and appoint trustees. As there were both Methodists and Presbyterians at the meeting

While men more often than not got the credit in the written record, it was the women of the community who were the driving force in religious affairs. About 1914 photographer (and choir member) Jim Dobbs of Dunchurch partially set the record straight by inviting the Ladies' Aid of the Dunchurch Methodist Church outside for a picture during a cleaning bee.

Courtesy of James A. Dobbs

they agreed to build a union church to be used for school purposes as well. So the site was chosen and the men got to work and cut the logs, put the building up, and roofed and floored it. They got a stove into it and some blocks and boards for seats, and it was considered ready for school. All they needed now was a teacher, so they thought Mr. Cooper, an old English gentleman just out from England, would just suit for the job…and the school was opened with a row of girls and boys sitting close together around the stove, holding books and slates in their hands. And Mr. Cooper undertook to make seats and desks while he taught us; he brought his tools and glue and put up a work bench at one side of the school. So he would give us a lesson and set his gluepot on the stove and go to his carpentering while we learned our lessons….

About this time, a depression of several years' duration stalled the lumber industry and dried up the only source of off-farm employment. Simultaneously, a grasshopper plague of biblical proportions descended upon the settlers' clearings, dealing them a double blow. Reuben Toye of the McKellar mission, writing in the Society's 1873–74 report, stated, "The past year with our people has been one of severe trial…destruction of their crops by the grasshopper and the failure of the lumber trade caused great destitution." In the same report, John Wilmott of Parry Sound noted that these conditions had caused some people to abandon the district, but he saw the lack of work in the woods as a partial blessing. In his view, the degrading lumber camp environment threatened to sap what remained of the community's manhood. "Young plants of piety," he lamented, "hardly ever survive such a wintering."

The appearance of union meeting houses kept pace with the advance of settlement, and some of them would serve for many years as a place of common worship. Over time, however, communities tended to stratify into denominations, and separate churches inevitably followed. Before the close of the century, the Scots of Dunchurch banded together to erect a Presbyterian church a stone's throw from that of the Methodists in the village's centre, while not much farther down the street stood the "English" church. The first regular clergymen were student ministers, for, as with schoolteachers, congregations could not afford the certified article. Thus, much of the preaching and teaching load was borne by laymen elders, such as "Deacon" Jonathan Crisp at Fairholme and William Robertson at Dunchurch, who in his broad Scots dialect once delivered from the pulpit the immortal line "led as a lamb to the slaffter."

When Rev. W.W. Walker arrived as a student missionary in Dunchurch in 1891, he found a Methodist church building and a parsonage of sorts awaiting him but no accommodation for his horse, which had to be stabled, at some expense, at a nearby hotel. Determined to rectify the matter but finding insufficient room on the property,

> *We went to the owner of the adjoining land, who gave as much as doubled the size of the parsonage plot without any coaxing on our part. Encouraged by this we at once went around among the people, one hardware man subscribing the nails, a lumber man the scantling and boards, another the shingles, etc. We then announced that work would commence on a certain day, and invited all the able-bodied men, who could do so, to be present to assist. At the appointed time several were on hand, and for days*

Christmas 1913 in John Hosick's lumber camp near Dunchurch. The men had to stay in the camp over the holiday because it was under quarantine, notice of which can be seen tacked to the door.

Courtesy of Ernie Carlton

missionary and people worked together from early morning until dark, the result of which was a fairly good barn, with one stall for horse, driving room for three rigs, and a loft that would hold three or four tons of hay.

In the beginning, the nearest source of medical aid for the Great North Road settler was Parry Sound, and even there, the attention of a qualified physician was not always to be had. In 1875, when a workman was seriously injured in his sawmill, the nearest doctor William Beatty knew of was Thomas Smith Walton, M.D., graduate of the Royal College of Surgeons in Edinburgh, who had abandoned the life of a ship's doctor for the dubious prospect of homesteading at the north end of Lake Joseph, 20 kilometres outside Parry Sound. Beatty got Walton to come and attend to the mill worker, and then prevailed upon him (little persuasion may have been necessary after six futile years of trying to transform 250 acres of Humphrey Township bush into an English gentleman's estate) to set up shop in town. He opened a practice, combined with a drugstore, on James Street, and until his death in 1902 was prominent in community affairs, serving as mayor of Parry Sound for three terms, and as superintendent of the Indian agency overseeing a number of reserves bordering on Georgian Bay. As a Conservative activist, Walton was constantly at loggerheads with Duncan Macdonald, secretary-treasurer of the Parry Sound–Muskoka Liberal Association, whose observations and opinions crop up frequently in this book. Such outside interests undoubtedly claimed some of the time and effort Walton might otherwise have devoted to his position as family doctor to both town and country. For whatever reason, he is said to have not been overly fond of making a house call outside the town limits, so settlers up the Great North Road continued to resort to local midwives for childbirth, and long, bumpy wagon rides for the seriously ill or injured.

Dr. Munro, who arrived in McKellar early in the 1870s, was probably the first physician to open a practice on the Great North Road.

Courtesy of John Moffat

In time, however, doctors set up practices in McKellar and Dunchurch, bringing health care closer to the people of the Great North Road. This was made possible in part by an early form of medicare administered by the lumber companies. In an 1897 issue of a Parry Sound newspaper, the Dunchurch correspondent noted that the local physician, Dr. O'Gorman, was at present visiting Sheehan's, Boyd's and Marshall's lumber camps, "where accidents occasionally happen in the way of cuts and fractures." Each employee's monthly wage was docked 25 cents (later increased to 50 cents) for a "doctor's fee," which was paid to the physician who had assumed responsibility for the men's health. He made periodic visits to each camp under his oversight, attending to anyone who was sick at the moment, advising management on disease and accident prevention

measures, and occasionally quarantining a camp when a contagious disease broke out. And if a lumberjack was seriously injured or contracted a lengthy illness, his hospital and doctor's bills were taken care of. This guaranteed income would have served as an incentive to a young doctor to locate in a backwoods place, and thus subsidized the care of the settler population, who had no such health insurance.

Two of these pioneering village doctors met untimely ends. In early November 1879, a certain Dr. Doupe and his bride of three weeks boarded the steamer *Waubuno* in Collingwood, bound for McKellar where the doctor intended to open a medical practice. Tragically, this was the legendary last voyage of the *Waubuno,* and the Doupes, together with everyone else on board, lost their lives when the vessel was wrecked among the Thirty Thousand Islands. Dr. William Ryerson Wade was an early — perhaps the first — doctor to settle in Dunchurch. Arriving there newly graduated in his mid-20s, he practiced family medicine and made regular rounds among a dozen or more lumber camps in the hinterland. When Hagerman Township was incorporated as a municipality, in 1890, Dr. Wade was elected as its first reeve and served until his death at age 32, in 1896. In those times, the general practitioner's lot included coping with periodic epidemics, and during an outbreak of diphtheria, Dr. Wade contracted the disease and died. That particular epidemic exacted a toll in property as well as lives. After 14-year-old William Wilson succumbed to diphtheria at the home of his grandparents, William and Mary Anne Moore near Dunchurch, government authorities ordered the "infected" house to be burned down, and compensation amounting to $50 was awarded to the Moores.

Dr. W.R. Wade, pioneer physician in Dunchurch and Hagerman Township's first reeve, died of diphtheria during an epidemic in 1896.

Most celebrated of the region's country doctors was Dr. James S. Freeborn. Although based in Magnetawan, his fast team of drivers placed the upper Great North Road well within range of his services. Freeborn opened his practice around the turn of the 20th century, and in a career that lasted into the 1930s gained a reputation for always being available no matter the hour or the condition of the road. Roy Cochran of Dunchurch phrased the public's opinion of the man as well as anyone:

> When anybody sent for Doc Freeborn he'd get there no matter how. He had a little team of blacks, and in the wintertime he had a cutter built like a toboggan and a sleigh, narrow runners and a bottom made like a toboggan. If the snow was deep it rode on top like a toboggan, and if the road was hard it rode on the runners. He was a very rough-speaking man but a very good doctor. And Doc Freeborn didn't care if you had five cents or if you had ten thousand dollars; the guy that had five cents, he treated him the same as the guy that had the money.

When George Dobbs of Dunchurch broke his leg playing at school, he remembered, after painful hours of waiting, seeing Freeborn pause as he hurried to their door to pluck two cedar shingles from where they were stuck in the garden to shade seedling plants. Freeborn quickly assessed the situation, then set the boy's broken limb using the shingles as splints, and only a teasing line of chatter as a sedative. In his historical sketch of central Parry Sound District titled *God's Country,* Rev. John Firmin cites an example of the determination this agent of mercy displayed in easing suffering, wherever it might lie:

> A heart-warming story came to me from one of the local residents. Dr. Freeborn had just returned from Ardbeg, a distance of 35 miles. Upon reaching Magnetawan, he found a very worried father, who lived over near Spence. A child was in need of the doctor's talents. Without stopping for so much as even a sandwich he jumped into his buggy, and gave the word to his already lathered horses to answer the call of a sick child. This, I am told, was par for the course for this most dedicated man.

CHAPTER NINE

Weddings, Shivarees and Booyaws

"THE NIGHTS SEEMED to be longer, then." So mused Johnny Sands, a grandson of Fairholme pioneer Joseph Sands, while reminiscing about the days of his youth, which bracketed the Great Depression when fun was hand-made out of whatever came to hand.

Johnny was referring to the fact that much of the excitement of those times seemed be associated with darkness and stealth. Then, Halloween offered no treat option, leaving the youngsters of the community free to devote the night to tricks, ranging from simple pranks like unhinging and hiding someone's front gate, to strategic maneuvers such as creeping into stables to lead away and "trade" farmers' horses, to highly complex undertakings like dismantling a wagon, hoisting its parts one by one onto a shed roof and reassembling it there.

Other long nights might be enlightened by a "booyaw" or a "shivaree." A booyaw (the name apparently derives from the French word for boiling) revolved around stealing a hen and stewing the carcass over a bonfire. Nowadays, after an evening of hanging out, a troop of hungry youths can resort to a nearby fast food

All music was of the homemade variety in 1910, as this picture, taken inside Buchanan's store in Dunchurch, illustrates.

Courtesy of
Harry Johnson

outlet to satisfy growling stomachs, but in the '30s such places did not exist, or certainly not up the Great North Road, so it was a case of starting from scratch by raiding a farmer's henhouse. Feeling his way along the roost in the darkness, the elected agent hefted birds until he found the heaviest, wrung its neck, and rejoined the gang who by now had a lard pail of water simmering over a fire in some out-of-the-way grove. By the time the tough old Plymouth Rock hen was plucked, gutted and rendered chewable, dawn might indeed be breaking. Johnny Sands could recount every booyaw he had taken part in, each one having some special character. Once, after an evening in the beer parlour, a neighbour offered to host one at his place, provided others did the foraging. The generous host never learned that the chicken came from his own henhouse. Another time, after fruitless attempts at other farmsteads, Johnny robbed his own roost rather than face the shame of returning empty handed.

Newlyweds Wilma Dobson and Stanley Ney swing out at their wedding dance in the Dunchurch agricultural hall in 1957 (bottom).

The father of the bride passes refreshments (below).

Rural marriages were commonly celebrated with a wedding dance, open to and hugely enjoyed by one and all. Couples who chose not, whether for religious or other personal reasons, to provide the community with what it regarded as its due, exposed themselves to the horrors of a "shivaree" (or charivari, as the dictionary prefers it). Mutterings among the cheated populace soon congealed into a plan of action, and late on the wedding night a crowd descended on the house

A wedding dance anywhere along the Great North Road meant a square dance. This is the orchestra and caller at the Dobson–Ney affair.

William Dobson, grandfather of the bride.

where the delinquent couple were assumed to be hiding. Some newlyweds made a considerable effort to avoid being found, but even if they left immediately on a honeymoon, which few then could afford, they might still be targeted on their return, for memories, like the nights, were long in those days. After creeping up in the darkness, at a signal from the leader the vigilante mob shattered the stillness with shouts and the clanging of cowbells and various other noisemakers. The end purpose of the custom seems to have been somewhat vague, but the first order of business was to persuade the couple to appear, hopefully in night attire, in a doorway or window. Sometimes that was enough; the crowd had had their revenge and a good snicker. Or, the cornered couple might relent and promise a dance at some future date, or invite the crowd inside for a cup of tea and whatever else the pantry might yield. Apparently the mob might even be bought off. In the April 25, 1879, issue of the *Parry Sound North Star*, the paper's McKellar correspondent leeringly noted, "We had a fashionable wedding last week. As the groom was 62 and the bride under 16 a charivari was expected, but the old gentleman nipped the fun in the bud by a timely fee of $2."

Occasionally, a shivaree might turn out to be fun for everyone involved. More than once, someone in the clamoring crowd took a closer look at the fellow hollering and ringing a cowbell in the dark beside him and discovered that the groom himself had sneaked out to join in the hoopla. More often, though, for the unfortunate couple it was simply harassment of the crudest kind.

Parry Sound social arbiter Duncan Macdonald left us a candid account of an early wedding celebration in a long and chatty letter he wrote, on March 31, 1884, to his political mentor and owner of the Parry Sound Lumber Company, John C. Miller, MPP. Miller, alas, would never read it, for as Macdonald wrote, Miller was dying of consumption in California. Fortunately, though, the 25-page letter was saved, for it documents in some detail all the social and political goings-on of the moment in and around Parry Sound. Here is Macdonald's take on a country wedding of the day:

Involving stealth and darkness, the shivaree did not lend itself to being photographed. Here, though, are pictures of one of the last of its kind, the victims of which were Dale Bloomer and his bride, Ardys (almost cut out of their photograph), American cottagers on Shawanaga Lake. The bride's father was the instigator, and he had no difficulty rounding up a few local men to carry it off. Cecil Crisp is carrying his deer rifle during the approach to the couple's hideout, then W.T. "Dub" Lundy and Lloyd Hosick commence the din by ringing a cowbell and pounding on a steel grader blade. All three men had been shivareed in their time, hence their enthusiasm.

They have had a big wedding in McKellar. Old "Bishop" McGee's daughter was married to Mat Leach of Parry Sound village. Rev. Mr. Mosely struck out on foot about 5 a.m. to the scene of operations. At Portage bridge they met him with a horse and cutter and made all haste back with him via Manitowaba Dam [Hurdville]. Well the knot was tied about 2 p.m. and they… had dinner. Bishop McGee presided on a packing case. At his right hand at the head of the table was planted a Five Gallon keg of Blue Ruin whiskey, and down the table was a fair supply of Bottled Ale and Claret, Sherry, Coffee, Tea and Cold water. The edibles were dealt with unmerciful and the fluids vanished like the summer snow. And the mirth and music fired up fast and furious. And about 4 p.m. the old Log Barn was turned into a dance room where they kept up the fun until sunrise next morning. About noon Mr. Mosely and the Parry Sound contingent arrived here pretty well used up and

Courting in style involved dressing up and going by buggy. Here, Bob Gibson and his friend Maggie Montgomery of Maple Island, have driven down to Dunchurch on a Sunday afternoon outing about 1916.

Courtesy of Norman Gibson

considerable worse of the wear, and the biggest and the loudest wedding that ever came off in the District was among the things of the past.

Also falling within the realm of romance was the box (or pie) social, a device craftily designed to exploit the male mating instinct in order to raise money for some worthy purpose. It was a form of "meet market," usually staged as a side attraction to some evening affair such as a concert or dance. All the young unmarried women brought baskets or decorated shoeboxes filled with enough sandwiches and sweetstuffs for two, and these were displayed on a table at the head of the hall during the main entertainment. Around 11 p.m., the auctioneer mounted the platform, picked up the first box and, after duly praising its artistry and the apparent attributes of its anonymous creator, began soliciting bids. Once the first bid was made and the ice was broken, the pace quickened, with the most heated action coming from just inside the hall door, where several unattached young bushworkers always lurked in hope of sitting next to a female for an hour, and indulging in some home cooking into the bargain.

The high point of the proceedings invariably came at the expense of some couple known to be "going together." When the boyfriend, tipped off as to which box to go after, started bidding, a conspiracy of his cronies joined in to make sure the embarrassed swain paid dearly.

Neither did this custom escape the notice of Duncan Macdonald who, in 1909, noted in his diary, "At night they held a pie social. The Schoolhouse was crowded. The Pie that took the cake sold for $2.80." At the other end of the Great North Road, Crystal (Cameron) LaBrash of Golden Valley, a granddaughter of the pioneering Whitehead family, vividly remembered a box social she attended in her teens. Deer hunting season, when the district swarmed with men from the south with cash in their pockets, was a good time to put on

British Empire ties coupled with a climate of seasonal employment made rural Parry Sound District fertile ground for recruiting campaigns, and in both world wars many sons and grandsons of the pioneers died overseas. Here, men of one company of the 162nd Battalion, raised in 1916, pose at the courthouse on James Street in Parry Sound.

a box social, and this was one of those. When a hunter she had never before seen bought her box, she was mortified, and barely managed to keep from fleeing the premises.

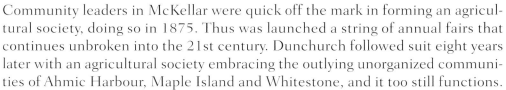

Pupils from five schools on parade in the Dunchurch fairgrounds about 1927.

Community leaders in McKellar were quick off the mark in forming an agricultural society, doing so in 1875. Thus was launched a string of annual fairs that continues unbroken into the 21st century. Dunchurch followed suit eight years later with an agricultural society embracing the outlying unorganized communities of Ahmic Harbour, Maple Island and Whitestone, and it too still functions.

The town of Parry Sound also hosted annual fairs into the 1930s, on grounds now occupied by the Parry Sound High School.

The autumn "Show Fair," a showplace for farm produce and home crafts of all kinds and an exhibition ground for travelling wonders from the outside world, was a highlight of the year for farm dwellers. Weeks in advance, men, women and older children began studying the annual prize list and planning what they would show. Hall exhibits were brought in a day in advance, while livestock followed in the morning, either herded along the public road (a challenge where a mixed lot of cattle and sheep were involved) or, in the case of pigs and poultry, caged aboard wagon or democrat. The livestock judging was a performance in itself, as the judge gravely poked, prodded and examined each beast before finally attaching the coveted red ribbon to the winner. At mid-morning, the door of the hall, within which other

Pupils of S.S. #1 Dunchurch school marching through the village to the fairgrounds in the 1920s.

Courtesy of George Buchanan

judges had been at work, was opened to admit a crowd eager to see what colours of ribbons graced their exhibits. And more than pride was at stake, for a family that really put its collective mind to the task stood to earn some real cash at a time when there was not a great deal of it in circulation. The promise of coins in the pocket (say 75 cents for a First in the milk stool category) was a powerful motivator for a boy. For a time, "School Fairs" were also held, a Saturday or two ahead of the "Big Fair." They opened with a parade of pupils from the various schools, and the exhibits included crafts and schoolwork prepared the previous June, plus livestock of the smaller variety. It was considered a coup to score prizes on the same halter-trained calf or birdhouse at both fairs.

At four o'clock, the livestock were loosed from pen and stall, and chased home by children counting and recounting in their heads the prize money that would soon be theirs, and the hall was magically cleared of every pie and piece of needlework in readiness for the square dance that always climaxed Fair Day.

Don Macfie training a calf to lead in preparation for showing it at the fair.

Courtesy of Edith Macfie

GOING TO THE TWELFTH

The Great North Road settlers were largely Protestant, and with Orangeism then a strong force in the province (for a time, Orange parades were banned by law in Ontario because of the Protestant–Catholic donnybrooks that sometimes ensued), lodges of the Orange Order sprang up in newly formed communities almost as soon as the first crops. Duncan Macdonald, whose multi-faceted career included a stint of newspaper reporting, witnessed the celebration of the Battle of the Boyne at McKellar in 1873, and wrote:

> The Glorious 12th of July was welcomed here by firing guns and small arms, flags waving from the various buildings, banners and bunting fluttering and flowing from the handsome arch erected across the street between the residence of Samuel Armstrong, Esq. and the McKellar House. At 7 a.m. the members of the L.O.L. 546 proceeded to the Orange Hall for their usual business and at 9 a.m. they formed into a procession and marched out to meet their brethren from Parry Sound and Waubamik. About 12 o'clock the procession of the day took place, marching to the martial music of fife and drum. First came L.O.L 546 composed of men from Croft, Hagerman, McKellar and Ferguson. Next came the Old Pioneers 170, true blues from Foley and staunch loyal men from McDougall. Last but not least came 783 from Waubamik, young and growing, all bound to do honour to the day Orangemen revere. With heads uncovered and hearts throbbing with enthusiasm…three cheers were given to the glorious memory of King William, and three more to the Queen. Then the procession marched to the "grove" where luncheon was prepared for all….

Keynote speaker that day was William Beatty of Parry Sound. Not an Orangeman himself (he said want of time prevented it), he nevertheless praised the movement at some length before closing with a subtle word of advice. Noting the fewness of Roman Catholics in the district, he then said, "How were we to act towards those we [have]? Were we to persecute them? No! Let us treat them rather like friends, like brothers, and if our object be to convert them, we shall thus stand a far better chance than by any other means. Persecution," Beatty declared, "is altogether contrary to the true principles of Orangeism." And mild persecution of Catholics, in the form of pranks and ridicule, was a fact of life on the Great North Road, and their fewness only served to increase the burden on the individual.

Lacking pressing issues on the religious front to deal with, the Loyal Orange Lodge found its real place as a fraternal organization and the host of the leading social and cultural event of the summer season. "We never missed 'The Twelfth'; wherever the Lodge was, we'd be there," Bella Dickie of Parry Sound recalled. Born in 1888 at Lorimer Lake as the only girl in the large family of Mr. and Mrs. William Charles Ferris, some of Bella's fondest childhood memories were of "going to the Twelfth," where her father and brothers, all tall, handsome fellows, would be on show. Typical was a turn-of-the-century expedition to Parry Sound:

Mr. and Mrs. William Charles Ferris and family, photographed while attending "The Twelfth" in Parry Sound. Daughter Bella is wearing a white blouse (the third woman is the wife of Bob, standing behind her).

We got up at three o'clock in the morning, got breakfast and got the boys ready for the Twelfth, got their suits ready. The men never waited on themselves, you know! Everything had to be just so; we had to sew straps on their pants. Then decorate the horses, the younger boys and I; braid up their tails and tie ribbons on them.... [Mr. Ferris and the older brothers] would go to McKellar in the big Peterborough canoe. I think the Lodge was supposed to meet there at six. They'd go down with the Lodge 'til they met us at Waubamik at nine o'clock. Mother and I and whatever boys were not old enough to be in the Lodge would drive to Waubamik, then drive down behind in all that dust, to Parry Sound. And march [beside] the Lodge all day....The parade started at one o'clock, and that's what I used to like, the lodges passing through one another.... We never thought of carrying lunches to the Twelfth. There was such a bunch of us we'd always go in and have lunch at one of the places putting up lunches.... We wouldn't get back 'til late at night — and have the cows to milk when we got home.

Chapter Ten

Changing Times

BETWEEN 1871 AND 1881, the population of Parry Sound District rose from considerably under 2,000 to approximately 15,000, and 10 years after that, the census revealed a population, outside the town of Parry Sound but within its sphere of influence, of some 24,500, about half of whom were living on farms. By now, the land rush up the Great North Road had subsided and the tide was about to turn. Waning soil fertility, the constraints imposed on additional land clearing by rock and swamp, and the rapid advance of lumbering operations ("When the pine is done, the country is done" was a common refrain of the day), had conspired to raise strong doubts about the future of farming in Parry Sound District. An 1885 issue of the *Parry Sound North Star* listed eight farms for sale between Parry Sound and McKellar. Asking prices ranged from $350 to $1,000, and assets typically included a log house (but sometimes just a shanty), a barn, and 15 or 20 acres cleared, with the balance of the acreage being "good hardwood bush."

Many homesteaders either abandoned the idea of farming altogether or joined a growing migration of agricultural settlers to the Canadian West. "Manitoba Fever" first appeared in the early 1880s, and rapidly became endemic. Those who succumbed to it were aided by settlement schemes promoted by the

The 1890s saw the start of a wave of re-migration of discouraged homesteaders to the West. Stephen Moore and his family, seen here at their home on Wilson Lake near Dunchurch, picked up and left to join "the Parry Sound Settlement" in Alberta.

Courtesy of Lyle Jones

Robena "Ruby" Harvey, one of the several children of George and Frances Harvey, photographed raking hay on her parents' small farm bordering on Owl Lake immediately north of McKellar. Like many other Great North Road settlers, the Harvey family joined the 1900-centred westward migration, and ultimately became widely scattered. Ruby became a nurse in Vancouver, and ended her days in California.

Courtesy of John Moffat

railways. There are farming communities throughout the West whose old families still trace their roots through one or another of the townships penetrated by the Great North Road. After enduring initial hardships, most of them prospered on their deep-soiled Prairie homesteads. In 1892, Arthur Millin of Dunchurch, the 54-year-old father of Mary whose memoir is quoted in this book, for the second time in his life pulled up stakes and, along with most of his now-grown children, heeded a call to a promised land. Some re-migrants simply abandoned their homes and clearings, particularly if they had not yet completed their settlement duties and obtained a deed. Others sold their holdings to a neighbour who planned to stay, or to a local merchant, about the only class of citizen who had the means to speculate in real estate. Around 1903, Willis Kenney clerked for a merchant in Dunchurch, and some 70 years later, described how the process — probably not an unreasonable one given the circumstances — worked. Kenney cited the example of a certain Whitestone settler who owed a substantial store bill, and who came into the store and announced that he was going West and wanted to sell out:

> Robertson went into the office and figured out how much he owed. "Yes, I'll buy your farm." They settled on a price, which must have been less than $1000, and Robertson says, "I'll give you $150 cash, and that leaves so much I owe you." And he says, "You'll need stuff to take with you, you're going out there and you've got to live." So he went through that store and he sold that fellow everything that had two ends to it.... He bundled up that stuff and gave him $150 cash, and the farm was gone.

One of those migrants was Peter Andrews, who, after 20 years homesteading with his parents in Hagerman Township, went to Alberta to join the "Parry Sound Settlement" then forming along the North Saskatchewan River near Edmonton. Following are excerpts from a letter he wrote on February 18, 1900, to David Patterson of McKellar, who also was considering pulling up stakes and moving elsewhere:

> *You asked me how I liked it living in this country, well I like it well and I would not think of going back to live there, I was there too long for my own good. I would say that this is the place for a man that intended to make his living farming. There was 50 bushels of wheat to the acre last harvest, and from 75 to 80 of oats, and I planted 6 bags of potatoes and I dug 145 bushels…horses is cheap…the cattle has lived on prairie all winter till now…. I got a nice piece broke on my place and I got the posts and rails out to put up my fence so I expect to have a crop next summer…. I am well satisfied with the country [but] would not like to advise anyone to sell and come less they would not do well…. If you think of coming you had better come and see for yourself before you sell….*

Many pioneering stories ended with a farm auction. The implements featured in this sale, which took place near Dunchurch in 1957, suggest that the farm did not make it out of the age of true horsepower.

As the number of farms along the Great North Road increased, the demand for produce in nearby lumber camps levelled off, prompting farmers to explore outside markets. Railways were seen as the key, so in 1875 John C. Miller, MPP for Parry Sound-Muskoka, headed a delegation to Queen's Park seeking assistance in having the Northern Railway, which by then had reached Gravenhurst, extended to Parry Sound. One of the delegates was Samuel Armstrong of McKellar, who, according to a report in the *Parry Sound North Star,* told the legislators that local farmers were growing "all kinds of cereals and root crops… and they were already producing a surplus of some articles, especially hay…." Furthermore, "with railway facilities to Parry Sound the population of the district would rapidly increase…. At present they had in winter to travel 70 to 100 miles to reach a railway…." However, it would be close to 25 years before the first railway, lumberman John R. Booth's Ottawa, Arnprior & Parry Sound line, which terminated at Depot Harbour on nearby Parry Island, approached Parry Sound, and still another decade before tracks of the Canadian Pacific and Canadian Northern Railways would actually enter the town. Periodic efforts were mounted to have a branch line connect Parry Sound and Burks Falls, paralleling the Great North Road as far as Dunchurch, but these came to nothing.

Following a visit to Dunchurch around 1896, Presbyterian missionary Rev. Angus Findlay wrote:

> The country is passing through a transient stage, the lumbering industry is pretty well completed, and nothing else has yet been found to take its place to supply ready cash…. When settlers take to dairying — for which their country is admirably adopted — times will improve permanently….

Opportunities for Parry Sound farmers to tap into outside markets were few. Here, members of the Little family of Trout Lake prepare to transfer three sleigh-loads of potatoes into a boxcar at Waubamik, around 1910.

Courtesy of Terry Little

DUNCHURCH, ONT.

Soon, a determined attempt was made to establish a dairy industry. While beef cattle would have to be driven long distances to tap into outside markets, cheese made from their milk, it was reasoned, might be readily exported. During the late 1890s, cheese factories sprang up in several district centres, the first one on the Great North Road being at McKellar. The Dunchurch Cheese Association, a co-operative formed about 1897, spent $400 erecting a building and equipping it with a boiler, vats and piping, then imported a cheesemaker from southern Ontario. The local agricultural society chipped in by financing the purchase of a purebred Ayrshire bull, with an eye to improving milk production. Farmer-patrons of the co-op living from Fairholme in the south to Maple Island in the north pledged to supply stated quantities of milk over the summer and fall cheese-making season. Farmers living at or near the far end of each route were paid to haul all the milk from that quarter. One of the McKellar plant's milk runs was performed by a small steamboat belonging to John Thompson, who delivered milk from Hurdville, at the far end of Lake Manitouwabing. In those days, whey, the watery by-product of cheese making, was customarily utilized by adding it to pig feed. The Dunchurch co-op turned pigs loose on a small island a stone's throw behind their factory (pigs are reluctant swimmers) and fattened them as a by-product.

In 1898, the Dunchurch factory produced nine tons of cheese, and the following year a foreign market was developed and briefly exploited, when an importer in Glasgow took two consignments totalling just over 100 cheeses and earning the enterprise about $900. The importer found fault with the construction of the round wooden boxes containing the cheeses, and noted that a few had heated while in transit, but otherwise found the product satisfactory.

However, from the beginning the Dunchurch enterprise was plagued with problems. Too many small plants (similar factories were also operating at Parry Sound, in Carling Township, and at Ashdown, near Rosseau) were competing for

Around 1900, an attempt was made to develop a dairying industry by installing cheese factories at McKellar and Dunchurch. The building erected to house the Dunchurch facility is on the extreme right. Following the cheese venture's early demise, the building served as a sawmill boarding house, a merchant's storehouse, a garage, a woodworking shop, a residence and a truant schoolboys' hideout before being destroyed by fire at mid-century.

Dunchurch Cheese Association, Limited.

We, the Directors of the above, beg to call the attention of the Shareholders and Patrons to the arrangements made for the season's operation.

A contract has been entered into with Mr. Alex. Anderson, of Rosseau, to run the factory for this season on the following terms: He buys the milk outright, paying 60c. at the factory, and patrons will be paid every month after the first two, season to last up to 31st October. Mr. Anderson's sole guarantee of milk is our list of cows promised, and all subscribers to this list are hereby requested to see that they fulfil their engagement, or at once shew to the Directorate reason for relief from same. As the drawing of the milk is to be shared equally by all parties, patrons will see the need of further-ing all effort to secure as large an amount of milk as possible; the prospects are that the drawing will cost considerably less than last year. Patrons are requested to make things as convenient as possible for the drawer, by having their milk on time on suitable stands along the highway. They are also warned to be careful of their milk, as to cleanliness, quality, etc., as Mr. Anderson ships direct, under his own name, to the Old Country, and is very particular.

The Directors take this opportunity of thanking outsiders who have promised their support, and Patrons who promised an increase on their first agreement.

The matter of the disposal of the whey is not finally settled, but it is not returnable in cans, and will likely be sold at the factory. In any case the milk is considered to be bought outright at the figure mentioned.

We are conscious that last season's operations were not very encouraging to a new enterprise, partly on account of the small quantity of milk supplied, also on account of the low price of cheese, but we fully anticipate that this year will be better, and that in that case the future success is assured, and we would solicit the hearty co-operation of patrons.

EDWIN TAYLOR,
President.

Two documents relating to the Dunchurch cheese factory venture.

Dunchurch June 2

Mr F A Mcfie.

Dear Sir.

I notify yous that the agerment I made with Mr Robertson was for 1 year which I did fullfill And he told one it would be no less than 40 & a hundred for the milk and I received very little more than 20 & and you can notify your milk man Mr Jas Sands that he nednt waste time stoping at my gate for milk and please let one know who put my name on any other agerment than for only the one year

Yourstruely

R Moore

a limited local demand, and shipping charges to the outside proved to be prohibitive. Moreover, farmers could not provide a reliable supply of milk because their cows usually "went dry" sooner than expected. In a desperate attempt to keep the enterprise afloat the directors of the association served notice on "backsliders" that they faced legal action if they failed to supply the milk they had promised. The response was as might be expected. Oliver Simpson of Fairholme dashed off a letter to the secretary announcing that he was turning his notice over to a lawyer, then in a conciliatory post-script, added, "If you take back what you said, I will burn the letter you sent me and there will be no more hardness about it."

In 1903, the Dunchurch Cheese Association wound up business and surrendered its assets to creditors. However, the cheese-making venture left its signature on the Great North Road for a good many years to come, in the form of dozens of covered milk can platforms standing wagon box-high on stilts, like vacant sentinel boxes marking each farm gate. Some of them would find a new purpose later on, when shipping cream to distant creameries became practicable and the weekly "cream cheque" began contributing to the farmer's cash flow. However small it might be during late autumn and winter (cows generally "freshened" in the spring, then produced milk for six or seven months), that cheque at least came regularly.

Land unsuited to agriculture was by no means wasteland. Almost every homestead had its sugarbush, and it took a great deal of firewood, another forest product, to keep a drafty pioneer home even tolerably warm. Any pine trees not used in building a house and barn belonged to the lumber company owning cutting rights on surrounding Crown land, but the company usually arranged with the settler that he would cut and deliver the timber to lake or river for an agreed price. At first, only the very best pine trees were wanted, those whose trunks were thick, sound and free of limbs for 40 or more feet and thus were suitable for hewing into square timber for the British market. If a settler found even four or five such outstanding specimens scattered over his lots he was in luck. In the hunt for those trees, property lines adjoining Crown land were sometimes found to be elastic, leading to an occasional case of poaching. As George Beagan phrased it, "They'd find an odd big pine away back in the bush, and in winter they'd snake it out over the beaver meadows." As a lad on a summer ramble, George happened upon a long line of weathered chips leading from a massive pine stump. He hurried home to report discovery of a place where an Indian of old must have carved out a dugout canoe. His father, Dan Beagan, replied, "I guess I was the Indian."

Land not worth clearing still grew trees, and a few hundred acres of bush could yield the farmer an annual cash crop of forest products in perpetuity.

Chopped down and hewed into squared sticks, then dragged to where they could be dumped into the water, the timbers earned the settler a welcome bit of cash when cash was rarely seen. Dave Wye, a son of Dunchurch pioneers, remembered seeing neighbours dragging a single piece of square timber down the Great North Road, with the forward end resting on a jumper or the front bob of a sleigh. There was a sharp bend in the road near Jordan Creek, and an extra long stick sometimes got stuck in rounding that corner.

All tree species other than pine belonged to the homesteader, and when the pine began to run out, hemlock and spruce, and most hardwoods — oak, birch, maple, elm, basswood and ash — gradually came into demand. In many instances the annual winter's harvest (logging was easier in winter, and other farm duties were then less pressing) of forest products yielded a larger cash return than did field crops and livestock. This kept the farm a viable enterprise considerably longer than would otherwise have been the case. Sawlogs were the main forest crop, but firewood for sale in town and village also contributed substantially to the Great North Road economy. So too did the bark of the hemlock tree.

Hemlocks were as common as pines in Parry Sound's primeval forest, often standing thick as cornstalks, their dense evergreen foliage excluding so much light that nothing grew on the ground below. Being high in tannin, pulverized hemlock bark was once used in the chemical bath in which animal hides were converted to tanned leather.

Winter work in nearby lumber camps for the man of the household kept many marginal farms going well into the 20th century. This gang, in Albert Atkinson's camp near Maple Island, is mostly made up of men living within a radius of 15 kilometres.

A commercial maple syrup operation in Hagerman Township.

Hemlock tanbark began to be harvested at least as early as 1879, when a shipment of 250 cords destined for Chicago was piled aboard a schooner in Parry Sound. Soon, tanneries were operating in Parry Sound–Muskoka, processing beef hides imported from as far away as South America. June, the hiatus between seeding and haying, also happens to be the season of the year when hemlock bark slips off the tree as easily as peel from a banana. Many farmers then headed for the bush to fell and peel hemlocks, either on their own land or for a lumber company. The bark was removed in four-foot sheets, sun-dried and piled on the spot, and later "swamped" out of the bush by jumper to where it could later be loaded on wagon or sleigh for the trip to the nearest railway siding or steamboat dock. Although hemlock lumber, being hard, heavy and brittle, is much inferior to pine, usually a market was found for the peeled trunks as well, in the form of sawlogs.

Roy Macfie piling hemlock tanbark.

It might be supposed that the surrounding wilderness would have provided settlers with a cash crop in the form of fur-bearing animals, yet early records make few references to trapping. (A rare handed-down anecdote concerns a trapper named Sharp, who periodically stopped in Dunchurch on his rounds. Then his visits abruptly stopped. Years later, loggers working near Long Arm of Whitestone Lake discovered a weathered human skull that was assumed to be Sharp's.) Considerable mention, however, is made of beaver *meadows*, natural clearings on low-lying land that formerly was flooded by beaver ponds, and now provided a welcome source of free hay in the form of a tall wild grass the settlers called "blue joint." Apparently beaver had once been common in the area, but were at a cyclical low in the latter half of the 19th century, and this resulted in a reduction of habitat for other pond-dwelling fur bearers such as mink, otter and muskrat.

John Sands checking a trap set for beaver.

A flurry of increased fur harvesting activity, spurred by high prices, occurred around the time of the Great War, but it was not until after the Second World War that trapping became a reliable profession, principally due to a return to abundance of beaver. At the same time, marten and fisher, two valuable fur-bearers that had long ago disappeared from the district (probably wiped out by the widespread use of poisoned baits to kill wolves), returned to their former habitat. Also at mid-century, the government instituted a refined set of trapping regulations that, by restricting licenses and imposing quotas, finally put wild fur harvesting on a sustained-yield footing.

John Sands and Bill Pugsley passing a large beaver lodge as they make the rounds of their trapline near Ardberg. Pugsley is carrying an otter.

◀○▶

By adapting to changing times and exploiting off-farm opportunities, succeeding generations continued to make a living on enough of the original homesteads to keep communities viable along the southern two-thirds of the Great North Road. Not so for the northern extremity, however. Soon after the Northern Railway reached Trout Creek, in the mid-1880s, the way outside for the Loring–Commanda axis of communities assumed an east-west orientation, and the arteries that first pumped life into them withered and died. So too did "the Hardscrabble," a name loosely applied to some settlers' clearings scattered along the road south and north of the Pickerel River. One of these clutches of homesteads, six or seven kilometres south of Golden Valley, prospered sufficiently to get its own post office, called Ardagh, but its life was brief. Norman Cameron,

Men not tied to farms were free to find work on the annual river drive. This gang of river drivers includes Waubamik men Harry Campbell (front row with his arms tightly folded), son of noted logging contractor Dougald Campbell, and on his left, his chum Charles Collison.

Courtesy of Ida Waddell

born at Golden Valley in 1894, described that section of the road as he remembered it from his boyhood:

> *The North Road came up from Maple Island. There never was a grain of gravel put on it, it was all clay. In the dry time of the summer, you could hike right along with a buggy, but when the fall rains came, it was bad. There's wagon wheels laying all along that road between here and Dunchurch. My granddad [James Whitehead] came up and cleared four acres back here in the Hardscrabble, then he had his wife and family come up from Hamilton. They were farming down there and heard tell of the pot of gold at the rainbow in the north, and came across to Parry Sound and up the North Road with the ox team, and started to farm. It was seven miles [from Whitehead's] down to Miller Lawson's place, where there was Miller Lawson and George Dawson, and a fellow name of Gould — three farms there. After Miller Lawson's, half way down to the Wildcat, was Charlie and Fred Lorenz's. They quit using that road, for the public to travel on, about 1912.*

In another taped interview, Pearl (Buchanan) MacLennan, another grandchild of James and Alice Whitehead, painted this picture of her forebears:

> *Grandma was Irish and he was Welsh and Irish, and they always said Grampa never needed braces; his hips was so big they held his pants up, and that's where we all got the big hips, Mother*

always said. They came from Wawanash Township, near Orangeville. Hughie Gibson took them up the North Road, a cow and a dog and five kids. Hughie moved a lot of people in, a three or four day trip. The father of the family usually came ahead and built the shanty; Grampa Whitehead did that, at the Hardscrabble. They built a log house after, but they lived in a shanty quite a few years. Sod roof. And a roothouse for the turnips and potatoes. They named their place Pansy Hills; the girls got picking pansies in the spring, and they named it Pansy Hills. They were four miles from Golden Valley, and it was opening up a little bit. There was a store at Commanda; they had a shortcut through, and that's where they got their groceries, flour and feed and stuff....

Little trace remains of Pansy Hills and the other homesteads along that lonely stretch of road; even the clearings are next to unrecognizable in the forest that reclaimed them. Kenneth Dawson, a son of George, put his father's experience in a nutshell:

> *My father was up the North Road in 1895 working in the lumber industry, and in a slack time he came back to Goderich and started courting a girl called Annie Dunkell. He married her and took her to the log house he built on the North Road. A child was born and died in infancy, then about 1905 his wife took ill. He*

A steam engine powers a rock crusher working beside the road in Parry Harbour.

*brought her out to Goderich and she died there. My father then
bought a farm near Goderich and never went back. He turned his
back on his house and farm on the North Road.*

Today, beyond the Ferrie River only a 5-kilometre-long tag end of the original
roadbed, where it approaches Commanda, remains in use. Evidence of the
balance — 30 kilometres or more — has largely disappeared into the floor of the
forest that reclaimed it.

◄○►

At the mid-point of the 20th century, some 1,500 properties were still
officially classified as farms in Parry Sound District as a whole, but how much
of the livelihood of the 6,000 people living on them was derived from the soil, is
open to question. By then, the provincial government was endeavoring to turn
back the clock by promoting reforestation of clearings won at great cost by the
pioneers. By the close of the millennium, only a handful of working farms
remained along the length of the Great North Road.

CHAPTER ELEVEN

There Were Giants in Those Days

L IKE THE ROBUST turnips that grew in the settlers' first clearings, the Great North Road also raised its crop of men of extraordinary might. Not far out of Parry Sound, near where the road crossed Portage Creek, stood the homestead of legendary strongman Charlie Reekie. In the woods, lesser men stood aside with their canthooks and watched in wonder as he wrapped his tree-thick arms around a sawlog to manhandle it onto a sleigh, just to show off. And on the river drive, he once picked up an anchor that took two ordinary men to lift, and tossed it easily into the water. The most oft-told Charlie Reekie story, handed down the years in several variations, and maybe purely apocryphal, involves him and his plough. In those days, word of men of exceptional prowess spread widely, and it was customary for them to seek out and challenge one another to a contest. One day a stranger came walking up the Great North Road, and on noticing a farmer working in his field, hailed him and demanded, "Can you tell me where the famous strongman Charlie Reekie lives?" "I can," replied Reekie, unhooking the horses from his plough. Hoisting the heavy implement by its two handles and pointing it toward his house, he declared, "I live right there!" At which his intended challenger muttered his thanks, turned on his heel, and marched back down the Great North Road.

Legendary McDougall Township strongman Charlie Reekie.

———◄◦►———

Had he so chosen, Aaron Teneyke of McKellar might have won the district's heavyweight wrestling or boxing championship with one massive hand tied behind his back. According to his son Burton, "He was six-foot-six-inches and weighed 275 pounds, and he didn't have a big stomach on him, and his mother told him to never hit a man." And evidently Aaron

The McKellar Township giant Aaron Teneyke held the rank of sergeant-major in the local company of the 23rd Northern Pioneers militia regiment prior to the Great War. He stands out in the middle of the back row in this photograph.

rarely did. Lumberjack Roy Cochran said of him, "Aaron Teneyke never was a man to pick fights, he was a peacemaker. He'd grab one man under each arm and walk away with them." Aaron instead made his name in other fields, notably as a fiddle player, an active Orangeman (he was County Master of the Orange Lodge for many years), and as a leader of men. When teenager Jim Canning first worked on the Seguin log drive, in 1888, his foreman was Aaron Teneyke. Jim told of descending Mountain Rapids with Aaron at the helm of a rowboat carrying the tents, the stove and all the cookery equipment, a scary experience for the youngster but all in a day's work for Teneyke. His son remembered that when Teneyke died, of a stroke at age 59, "they got a coffin in [Parry Sound] and it wasn't long enough, so they had to order a new one. My father was a big man, you know."

—◄○►—

Further yet up the Great North Road, at Maple Island, lived John Brear. Born (as Jean Briere) in Quebec in 1851, he followed the square-timber trade west out of the Ottawa Valley and over the height-of-land to where it finally petered out, in the Georgian Bay watershed. There, in the late 1870s, he took up a homestead along the Great North Road immediately south of the Ferrie River, and married neighbour Ann Ward, remembered as the ever-dependable midwife of the community — and the mother of 13 Brears.

A muscular six-footer, Brear also gained notice for such Herculean feats as routinely hoisting a 100-pound sack of flour on his back to carry it home from Dunchurch, and once, on a bet, lugging a 600-pound barrel of pork over that village's bridge (which happened to be close by the Dunchurch's liquor hotel). His real prowess, though, lay with the broad axe, the specialized tool that shaped the storied square-timber era of logging. He plied his trade at Maple Island until the British-based square timber market dried up, before turning to homesteading and general bush work. However, there remained a need for hewers to square up the timbers that went into log homes and timber-frame barns, and the dams that lumbermen installed to manipulate water flow during the annual log drive. For years, Brear filled this role around Maple Island. In the process, people took note of his expertise with the broad axe, and some were given to flights of fancy in describing it. Here is an example, in the words of Nelson Clelland, a life-long resident of Maple Island:

At picnics, everybody had to show what they could do, races and one thing and another. John Brear always took the prize for hewing timber. So some of them thought they were going to pull one off on John. They brought in an expert, and he hewed this piece of pine perfect in every way. They said John Brear couldn't do that. John must have heard about it, for he didn't come to the picnic at first. Well, when they was all looking at this nice hewing they heard somebody whistling, and here was John coming with his broad axe over his shoulder. They said, "Well, John, you're beat this time." John looked around, and there was a fellow reading the Family Herald. He says, "Say, could you give me a sheet of that paper?" John takes the piece of paper and plasters it on the side of the square log with some pine gum, and gets it all smoothed up. He whets up his axe, then comes down once with it, and puts it on his shoulder and walks away. They went over, and what do you suppose had happened? He hewed the print right off that paper!

A master of the hewing axe, John Brear followed the square timber trade over the height-of-land from the Ottawa Valley to the Magnetawan River watershed, then homesteaded at Maple Island.

Courtesy of Andy Houser

While no giant in the physical sense, Dougald Campbell of Waubamik looms large in Parry Sound logging lore as a capable and colourful bull of the woods. Each winter he contracted with a lumber company to harvest the season's cut of timber, and then each summer to float the thousands of sawlogs downriver to Georgian Bay.

Courtesy of Dan Campbell

When Richard Cooper of Dunchurch died in 1959, Dr. K.A. Denholme, a highly respected physician and community leader in Parry Sound, was moved to compose an obituary that measured the man this way:

Dick Cooper knew the district in a way that few of us do. He knew treachery and cruelty of the winter bush and wilds. He knew the river driving in the swollen waters of the springtime. He knew life in the lumber camps and lumber mills. He knew where every fish could be found. He was on good terms with the deer and bear and animals of the forest. Hunting season was the most precious time of the year, for him. He was like the village blacksmith of Longfellow's poem, with his great strength and his great gentle and good heart.

I couldn't have said it better, and in my youth I knew Dick very well. He was a grandson of a pioneer settler, also named Richard, who homesteaded about two kilometres south of Dunchurch. Older residents still refer to the section of the Great North Road fronting this property as "Cooper's Hill," even though improvements to Highway 124 long ago eliminated the hill and Richard the First's stay there was brief. He soon abandoned his rocky location and moved to Dunchurch, where he served as the village's first schoolmaster, making the room's furnishings as he taught.

His grandson, the Richard I knew, was equally handy with his hands, which, though approaching hams in size, rendered him anything but ham-handed. One of his many talents was divining for subsurface water, and I once watched in awe as the stout willow "witching" crotch shred at his tightly clenched fists as it warped downward to indicate a run of water somewhere below. Dick ran logging camps, blacksmithed, and built buildings and rowboats and anything else that could be fabricated from wood. One day when I was out with him on a deer hunt, he paused beside a well-proportioned ironwood tree, lovingly stroked its scaly trunk and declared, "That'll make dandy axe handles," then chopped a blaze in its side for future reference. A lot of my deer hunting experience was gained in Dick's wake. It was hard training because whenever a rocky ridge came between him and where he was going he simply charged over the top instead of taking the easy way around. Where others might

Dougald Campbell's fine home stood as a landmark close beside the Great North Road in Waubamik. In it, he and his wife raised 13 children, including a flock of boys who followed him into the lumber woods. Dougald played the fiddle, and the spacious front room of his home, which held a piano, was often the scene of an impromptu square dance.

Courtesy of
Henry Campbell

wait for help to drag it out of the bush, when Dick bagged a deer he dressed the animal then draped it over his massive shoulders to carry it over the hills and through the swamps as if it was a sack of feathers.

Some people dismissed Dick Cooper as an individual who did things the hard way out of bull-headedness. Others, like Ernie Carlton of Parry Sound, knew him as a man of direct action. When Ernie was a novice lumberjack he slashed a foot badly with an axe, at which Dick hoisted him on his back like a deer and carried him two miles out of the bush. This side of Dick Cooper's nature is best illustrated by the time, around 1920, when in High Noon fashion he planted himself in the middle of the Great North Road in Dunchurch to bar the path of three ruffians bent on escaping justice by catching a steamer at Ahmic Harbour. Cooper engaged all three in a one-sided fight that left him brutally beaten. Vigilantes later cornered the trio and held them until police arrived, but Cooper was left with the imprint of brass knuckles in his skull and a voice rendered permanently husky by a kick in the throat.

Dick Cooper, raised in hard times, liked to boast that he survived one long-ago winter eating nothing but turnips. I wonder whether he was strong in body and character in spite of, or because of, hard times and turnips. Considering those glowing reports about the size and quality of the turnip crops grown in the settlers' first clearings, I am inclined to believe the latter. A monument to the man stands close to the Great North Road in the form of several tourist cabins he built on Whitestone Lake during the guiding and outfitting phase of his multi-faceted career. Firmly founded on fieldstone underpinnings, the cottages, just downstream from the bridge in Dunchurch, still welcome vacationers to the surroundings Dick Cooper knew so intimately and loved so dearly.

Bobby Orr.

Beyond question, the most widely renowned individual to qualify for this pantheon of men of mighty accomplishments is Robert Gordon Orr, better known both within and without hockey circles as Bobby Orr. His childhood home on the Great North Road in Parry Sound's east ward hugged the street so tightly that whenever the young phenomenon stepped out the door on his way to the skating rink or the ice of the Seguin River just across the railway tracks, he stepped directly onto it. The story of hockey legend Bobby Orr is so deeply etched in the Canadian landscape that it needs no elaboration here. Suffice it to say that it started right here at 24 Great North Road, barely half a kilometre from where that thoroughfare began its own historic journey.

Above: Bobby Orr, the Great North Road's most illustrious citizen.

Middle: Native son and Boston Bruins star Bobby Orr, along with Bruins goaltender Eddie Johnston, acknowledge the crowd on Parry Sound's James Street during Bobby Orr Day in 1970.

Bottom: The childhood home of hockey legend Bobby Orr stands on the other side of the Great North road.

Courtesy of
Jack Thompson

CHAPTER TWELVE

Seizing Power: Industry and Enterprise

AULING LUMBER FROM Parry Sound into the forested interior for home and barn construction was akin to carrying coal to Newcastle, so it followed that in every community someone would seize the opportunity to install a sawmill to supply local needs. If a stream with a fall of water worth harnessing was handy, that was utilized, and if not, a steam boiler and engine would be imported and set up. The first such enterprise outside Parry Sound itself was that of a pioneer settler, possibly Louis Stillar, who installed a water mill at the outlet of Harris Lake at Waubamik, to make lumber for local consumption. In 1871, Paul Leushner, an Austrian-born watchmaker with a practice in Cookstown, Ontario, succumbed to an urge to be a landholder and came north to locate 200 acres at the north end of Harris Lake. For a while, he maintained his business in Cookstown, making periodic excursions to Waubamik to clear land. Perhaps the machinery of the mill at the foot of the lake, not unlike a gigantic piece of clockwork, appealed to the watchmaker. Anyway, he abandoned his farming plans, acquired the mill, and thereafter derived his living from it, supplemented by watch repairing on the side. In 1903, his son, Fred, took over the mill and ran it

Paul Leushner at the controls of his water-powered sawmill at Waubamik.

for another decade before moving to Toronto. Today, the idle millsite serves as a summer resort for the current generation of Leushners.

The docile appearance of Harris Lake Creek where it crosses beneath Highway 124 just north of Waubamik belies the fact that for 40 years it turned the heavy machinery of a sawmill. In truth, for much of the year the sluggish stream was incapable of doing so. Harris Lake sits at the top of a minor branch of the Seguin River, so the water supply was fitful at best. A wood and earth dam super-

imposed on the rapids at the outlet provided a 10-foot head of water. A flume set in a channel blasted out of bedrock carried water down to a turbine, from which a shaft arrangement transmitted power to the sawmill, sitting close beside the dam. An endless chain, also drawing power from the turbine, dragged each log from the lake, ready to be rolled onto a carriage and rendered into lumber by a huge circular saw.

Del Leushner with the turbine and power takeoff shaft of his grandfather's mill at the outlet of Harris Lake.

An account book kept by Fred Leushner reveals how tied to the mercy of the weather a water-powered mill was. The annual sawing season began with the early-April spring freshet, and tapered off rapidly after the end of May, when runoff was finished and the reserve of water held by the dam was exhausted. Occasional rainy spells yielded sufficient water to run for a day or two here and there in late summer and fall, and those rare occasions when the mill was started up in January or February mirror mid-winter thaws of unusual proportions. A sawmill is a cold, drafty place to work in winter, but to a miller on a small stream, allowing any water to rush downstream unharnessed was like watching life's blood flow unstaunched.

The Leushner mill, in spite of its slight source of energy, was no plaything. Ledger entries show it could turn out as much as 5,000 board feet of lumber in a day (undoubtedly a day that took advantage of every hour of daylight and every cubic foot of water), and during April and May 1905, about 75,000 feet of custom

After learning the lumber trade from the ground up working for major companies, James Ludgate launched his own successful enterprise early in the 20th century, starting with this sawmill in McKellar, which he operated in partnership with Herb Thompson. In 1919, Robert Harvey assumed ownership and ran it until it was destroyed by fire in 1943.

sawing was done, in addition to any logs of his own that Leushner might have processed that season. When the Toronto–Sudbury line of the Canadian Northern Ontario Railway reached Waubamik, it gave access to outside markets. In 1909, Leushner shipped 90,000 feet of pine lumber to a dealer in Toronto, and other documents reveal negotiations with a firm in far-away Buffalo for a consignment of hemlock. Paradoxically, even such giant lumber producers as the Parry Sound and Peter companies in Parry Sound, and the Graves, Bigwood Company at Byng Inlet, placed small orders with Leushner, likely for building lumber camps in the interior north and east of Waubamik.

"Grievous Bob" Moore in his blacksmith shop that long stood as a landmark close beside the Great North Road.

Courtesy of Macil Moore

◄○►

The Free Grants and Homestead Act gave the homesteader the unencumbered privilege, once certain settlement conditions were met and title was granted, of living upon and tilling the soil, but not the right to everything on and under it. The government retained ownership of all pine trees not used in construction or removed during land clearing, and "all gold, silver, lead, iron, or other mines or minerals" were likewise reserved as property of Her Majesty. The abundance of outcropping bedrock in the Ottawa-Huron tract no doubt led the government to expect that many mines would be discovered there, and it wanted to retain the privilege of profiting by them. In truth, the geological province encompassing the region would gain notoriety in mining circles for the wide range of valuable minerals found there — and for the fact that, in 150 years of searching, remarkably few occurrences would ever prove to be sufficiently large and concentrated to constitute commercial orebodies.

A transparent form of mica known as Muscovite, once used in manufacturing (for example as window panes in stove fronts) occurs widely in the region penetrated by the Great North Road, and sporadic attempts were made to exploit several of the occurrences. However, none ever proved to be commercially viable.

In his introduction to the 1879 *Guide Book and Atlas of Muskoka and Parry Sound Districts*, W. E. Hamilton, speaking of Dunchurch, remarked on "a smooth and beautiful rock, owned by Mr. Kelcey, near the Narrows, which has all the appearance of the whitest Carrara marble." This outcropping, which gave Whitestone Lake its name, was indeed marble, and although too coarse-grained and impure to warrant a second look from a Michelangelo, it would prove to be the most useful mineral found along the Great North Road. A crystallized form of limestone

A sample of the crystalline limestone that gave Whitestone Lake its name, and provided settlers with lime for chinking the cracks in log homes.

occurring in a discontinuous belt running up the middle of Parry Sound District, it was exploited as a source of lime for mortaring stone foundations and brick chimneys, chinking cracks in log homes, and plastering and whitewashing their interiors. In each community blessed with a limestone outcropping, someone built a kiln and produced lime as a sideline, selling the finished product for 25 or 50 cents a bushel (there is no record of the government ever having attempted to collect a royalty on these minor mining ventures). The top of the kiln was filled with broken chunks of the crumbly stone, beneath which a wood fire was maintained for about a week before the carbonate component was driven off and the mass collapsed into a heap of lime. The practice of "killing" lime pretty much died out by the second decade of the 20th century, but the tumbledown remains of old fieldstone kilns can still be found here and there, hidden amid clumps of lime-loving brush and trees.

THRASHER JACK AND THRASHER JOHN

The pioneers' principal cash crop was oats. This grain flourished in the new clearings, and a ready market existed in nearby lumber camps, but first the harvested crop had to be threshed. Initially this was done the hard way, by spreading a few sheaves on the "thresh floor" of the barn, pummeling them with a flail, and shoveling up and winnowing the resulting mass of dislodged seeds and husks on a breezy knoll.

For decades Jack Moore served as thresherman for a wide area surrounding Dunchurch, employing steam-powered equipment. When the internal combustion engine took over he still enjoyed making the autumn rounds as an elder statesman of the profession. Here, from the shade of a convenient tree, he watches a threshing in Sunny Slope in the 1950s.

Gradually, the winnowing chore was handed over to crank-operated, factory-made fanning mills, which, come spring seeding time, also cleansed seed grain of weed seeds. In 1880, *The Parry Sound North Star* noted the arrival in McKellar of what presumably was the first travelling threshing outfit to visit the region, a "Paragon" model manufactured by "the celebrated Abel's works, Woodbridge." It would have run on natural horsepower generated either by teams of horses hitched to arms radiating from a central gear arrangement, or by horses plodding in a treadmill that similarly transmitted energy to the grain separator by belt and pulley.

"Thrasher" John Hosick pioneered custom threshing at Dunchurch around the turn of the century, when he acquired a small grain separator and treadmill and began touring surrounding farms after harvest time. In 1910, "Thrasher" Jack Moore, another enterprising son of pioneer stock, took matters a step further by bringing in a steam engine and a threshing machine with a substantially larger capacity than Hosick's. Both engine and separator were horse-drawn, and the top-heavy engine in particular was awkward to handle on the road. Once, it upset completely, and another time the poor horses were all but overrun as the behemoth charged uncontrolled down the Grange Hill into Dunchurch. Moore expanded the Dunchurch threshing circuit to encompass the Great North Road from Fairholme to Maple Island, including three or four sideroads, a territory supporting 20 or more active farms. Staying abreast with the times (actually one step behind, for the world outside was now going over to gasoline power), around 1930 Moore upgraded his outfit with a steam traction engine, and thereafter moved from farm to farm self-propelled at approximately one mile per hour.

Around the turn of the century, Peter Harvey introduced McKellar farmers to the steam age of threshing. Robert Moffat's grain crop, stored in sheaves in a mow of his barn, is being put through the separator on the thresh floor, while straw piles up beyond the far door.

Courtesy of John Moffat

Arthur Buchanan.

Courtesy of Macil Moore

Challenging church and school as the community's centre of gravity was the village general store. Both a seller of settler's needs and a buyer of products of the farm, it certainly was any settlement's commercial hub. Typical was Arthur "Art" Buchanan's store in Dunchurch. Buchanan came north from Goderich, Ontario, in 1886 at 19 years of age. His father, who had preceded him to Dunchurch, was running a small shoemaking business in a log cabin that had been the village's first home, that of Arthur Millin and family. Young Art took over the shoe-making enterprise and expanded it, tapping into a market waiting in a score of lumber camps dotting the hinter-land. Demand was brisk for shoepacs, a moccasin-like form of winter footwear, and for river drivers' calked boots. Meanwhile, he began building larger premises in the village centre, and in due course moved his shoe-making business there, and set up shop as a general merchant. Typical of the times, this included not just selling groceries, hardware and drygoods, but dealing in farm machinery, sleighs and wagons, livestock, and buying hides and furs. A barbershop, the domain of Art's brother William, was squeezed into a corner, and in another room their sister, Nellie, ran a dressmaking business. As other opportunities presented themselves, Art exploited them. When migration to the West got underway in the 1890s, real estate suddenly became a paying commodity. Migrants traded their homesteads, often at fire-sale prices, for an outfit and a small stake of cash for the journey. When the CNR line was being built through Ardbeg, Art supplied contractors with the groceries and meat needed to feed their men.

In late winter Art Buchanan engaged a fleet of sleighs to fill his warehouse with a carload or two of goods delivered by rail to Waubamik or Boakview. The large pile of firewood on the left likely would have been taken in as credit on settlers' store accounts.

Courtesy of Marshall Dobson

A shipment of 37 deer purchased by Art Buchanan from local hunters about 1913, and destined for the Harris Abbatoir in Toronto. Buchanan is holding the rifle, while his clerk and ultimate successor, Jim Dobbs, is on the extreme right.

Courtesy of
James A. Dobbs

A good deal of the store trade was in barter. Fuel-wood, wool, dressed hogs and deer, cattle and sheep on the hoof, and of course housewives' butter, eggs and knitting, all helped pay down the store bill. Raw wool was sent to the Bird Woollen Mills at Bracebridge and was returned as yarn, mackinaw and blankets to stock the store's shelves. Supplies came in from the railhead at Burks Falls by Magnetawan River steamboats in the navigation season, and in winter by team and sleigh from Parry Sound (and following the opening of the Canadian Northern Ontario Railway in 1908, from Boakview). After little more than a decade in business, Art Buchanan was, according to a news report, "worth $30,000 to $40,000 without any encumbrance." Although R.G. Dun & Company's Mercantile Agency Reference Book for 1913 ranked Buchanan's "estimated pecuniary strength" only in the $5,000 to $10,000 bracket, it is still quite a success story for one who started with no merchandizing experience and, as he himself liked to boast, just $13 in capital.

Prosperous citizens were expected to give back to the community, and Art Buchanan did so. Hailed during his lifetime for his involvement in civic and social affairs — a term as township reeve, sponsor of agricultural society activities, superintendent of a Sunday School, and supporter, always leavened with a sense of humour, of "any scheme for the benefit of the community." It came as a blow to the district when he died in 1921, at age 56.

One day in 1906, a village youth named James A. Dobbs entered Buchanan's store on an errand for his mother. Needing casual help around the place, Buchanan offered the lad part-time work in the store, Dobbs accepted, and in 1910 the job became permanent. On Buchanan's death, Jim Dobbs stayed on to run the store, then assumed ownership on the death of Mrs. Buchanan in 1927. Years before, Dobbs's father, sawmill-owner and builder Thomas Dobbs, had assumed the duties of mortician for the area, manufacturing coffins in his workshop and attending to the "laying out" and burial of the dead. On taking over the Buchanan enterprise, Dobbs turned the second storey of the store into a funeral

Buchanan's store in Dunchurch.

Courtesy of George Buchanan

parlour, and, in addition to filling the role of friendly village storekeeper, carried on as undertaker and coffin-maker (average price: $15) for another 30 years, during which, with due dignity, he conducted scores of his fellow citizens to their final resting places.

When advancing age forced Dobbs's retirement, his store closed its doors and was long ago demolished. But it still stands as a major landmark in memories of my youth, which I suppose explains why it is featured in this book. In keeping with long-established tradition, Wednesday and Saturday nights were open nights for country stores, and as soon as we grew old enough (around age 10) to tackle the seven-mile round trip, one or two of my brothers and I invariably struck off on foot for Dunchurch each Wednesday and Saturday as soon as the evening barn chores were done. There was always some practical purpose to the trip — mail to be got or posted, or the gallon coal oil jug to be refilled, or some small grocery order to get — but for us youngsters it was a social activity, an early form of "hanging out." We might hike all the way to Dunchurch with just each other for company, but in the course of going from store to store calculating how to best spend the nickel or dime in our pockets (Dunchurch then boasted two general stores plus two or three smaller places selling confectionary and such) and falling in with friends, a small crowd of cohorts usually coalesced. This made the long trudge home easier, for the energy generated by the banter and horseplay both lightened the darkness and, on a sub-zero winter nights, warmed the air, particularly those rare times when the gang included a couple of girls.

It was around the winter of 1938–39 that Dobbs's store got me hooked on Saturday night broadcasts of Toronto Maple Leafs hockey games. I never actually laid eyes on the radio that brought Foster Hewitt's play-by-play into the store, for the set was somewhere in the Dobbs's living quarters that occupied half of the lower storey of the building, but the volume was turned up high enough for it to be heard clearly in the store. I don't know whether Jim was a hockey fan, or if he just used the broadcast to attract and hold customers, but once I had formed a reasonable mental image of the action on the ice of Maple Leaf Gardens, the mystique of the Toronto Maple Leafs certainly held me — and has yet to entirely let go. The building's electricity source was a gasoline-powered Delco generator whose single sparkplug produced an explosive burst of static over the radio with each firing. Foster Hewitt's frantic play-by-play thus entered the store filtered through a screen of staccato noise, but the insistent background beat seemed merely to heighten the excitement of being there as Leaf captain Syl Apps wristed another one behind the hapless Boston Bruins or New York Americans goalkeeper.

Chapter Thirteen

Crime and Punishment

MUCH HAS BEEN made of how the lowly lumberjack resorted to fisticuffs to avenge an injustice or perceived slight, but thanks to Duncan Macdonald's writings, which provide a ringside commentary on one such confrontation, we know that industry bosses also were not above settling accounts with their bare knuckles. In this case the antagonists were John McClelland, manager of the Parry Sound Lumber Company, and logging contractor Mat Rankin, individuals who, Macdonald remarked in a letter to John C. Miller, owner of the Parry Sound Lumber Company, "have not loved one another beyond the bounds of common decency for the past two years." Matters came to a head on Seguin Street in Parry Sound one March day in 1884 in front of McClelland's office, on ground now occupied by a shopping plaza. Rankin, whose son had cut some logs in Foley Township for the lumber company and was now ready to start floating them downstream to Parry Sound, came to see McClelland about merging them with another lot of company-owned timber to make a single, more economical drive of it. Seemingly Rankin Sr. had built dams and timber slides on the stream (evidently in the Boyne River watershed), and thus felt he had a proprietary interest in it. The price McClelland offered for bringing down the additional logs fell short of Rankin's expectations, leading to hot words that ended with Rankin declaring, "I have a great mind to kick you!" McClelland laughed and turned to re-enter his office,

> …and as he got the thumb latch in his hand Mat raised him on the Blind with his boot…. The long wished for moment…was there, and Mac embraced the opportunity by drawing up and striking Mat between the eyes and knocking him clean off the platform onto the street. Mat came up smiling, and squaring off, he planted a body blow on Mac's shoulder. Mac sailed in and grabbed Mat by the beard and throat and showered in his blows fast and furious around Mat's nose, mouth and eyes, then giving him a push away from him. Mat fell in the wet sand and sawdust, a blind, bruised, bleeding, dazed, senseless used up community. Some of his friends led him [across Seguin Street] to Billy Taylor's shoe shop where they washed him and led him up to Dr. Walton's for repairs.

Shooting victim Thomas Jackson of Waubamik.

When a fusillade of automatic pistol shots shattered the pre-dawn stillness of Waubamik on August 18, 1928, it triggered a flood of attention from the nation's big-city newspapers, ushering Parry Sound into crime's big league and stripping it of its innocence. The incident remains the most sensational Great North Road story of all time. The pulp detective story magazines of the day called it the "Great Parry Sound Train Robbery," but all up and down the road a saga that began the previous evening on a Toronto-bound passenger train and ended tragically several hours later in a roadside ditch at Waubamik, would enter local legend as the "Shooting of Thomas Jackson." It was a time — the close of the Roaring Twenties decade — when daring criminal acts coupled with gunplay and getaway vehicles came into prominence, and this episode featured all three elements.

The melodrama began when two masked and armed men robbed the mail car of an eastbound Canadian Pacific Railway passenger train of several thousand dollars' worth of cash and valuables, and then, as the train pulled into the Parry Sound station, leaped out into the early morning darkness. Around 3:00 a.m., the sound of grinding gears awakened members of the Laird household on Gibson Street. Discovering that a Buick coupe belonging to a brother-in-law visiting from Ohio was missing from the yard, 24-year-old Walter Laird and his younger brother, Haughton, persuaded H.J. Roland, an employee of the Laird family's jewelry store who owned a car, to drive them in pursuit of the stolen vehicle.

The car's tracks, visible in the rain-moistened gravel, led straight out of town and up the Great North Road. Just beyond Waubamik, where the road curved sharply in its approach to the bridge over Harris Lake Creek, lived

In the 1920s identical concrete bridges were installed at various points between Parry Sound and Dunchurch. This one at Waubamik made the national news in 1928 when the Laird brothers blocked it with a car before capturing fleeing mail car robber John Burowski.

In image: Where Jackson was shot X

Photographed Aug 19-29

Thomas Jackson, a 62-year-old farmer. Jackson had arranged with a neighbour to go blueberry picking that Saturday, but he would not live to see it dawn. Roused by a motorist seeking a tow, Jackson and his son Claude gave the man a chain, then harnessed a horse and followed him to where a speeding automobile had failed to negotiate a curve in the road and ended up in the ditch. The stranger, evidently unfamiliar with automobiles, had hooked the chain to a tie-rod, so that when the horse pulled, the front wheels turned crosswise, further miring the vehicle.

At that moment, the pursuing Laird brothers arrived on the scene. Racing back in the darkness after blocking the bridge with their car, they found the younger Jackson busy with the horse in the headlights' glare, the father at the rear, and a third man sitting in the driver's seat. Walter Laird ordered him to get out, which he promptly did, but on the opposite side of the car. Walter confronted him and a fusillade of automatic pistol shots ensued, some of which were clearly fired by the man he quickly pinned to the ground, others of which seemed to come from the nearby bush. One bullet wounded Walter in his left side, another apparently ricocheted off the car and struck Thomas Jackson, who was holding a lantern to illuminate the scene, in the throat. With Walter on top of the gunman and forcing his .45 Colt automatic pistol into the mud, Haughton Laird knocked him senseless with a wrench brought from the pursuit car. While running to the house to telephone police and find a rope to tie up the bandit, Claude Jackson came upon his father lying dead in the lane, drowned in his own blood.

Police detectives at the spot where Thomas Jackson was shot, after a car speeding up the Great North Road took the ditch and he and his son came to the rescue with a horse to pull it out. The Jackson farm is in the background.

Archives of Ontario/RG 23-35 William H. Stringer scrapbook

Police "mug shots" of John Burowski, who was hanged for the shooting of Thomas Jackson.

Courtesy of Ontario Provincial Police Files

Two police officers and the coroner arrived to find the gunman in the Jackson home, bound with rope and guarded by his captors. The prisoner identified himself to the lead officer, Constable Robert Beatty, as John Burowski, a carpenter from Toronto. Evidence collected later suggested that this was merely the alias of a gangster on the run from the law in the United States. If this was so, it was hardly a wise choice of name for use in an overwhelmingly Wasp district like Parry Sound. Not that the fellow had much hope, anyway. When captured he had $1,800 in cash on his person, which he first tried to give to Walter Laird while the latter held him pinned in the mud, then to Claude Jackson, claiming he wanted to pay his father's funeral expenses. More likely, though, it was a combined bribe offer and attempt to dispose of the incriminating evidence. Baggage car mail clerks identified Burowski in a police line-up, his bandana mask reportedly having slipped from his face during the holdup, but he was never charged with the heist, apparently because the Crown attorney believed he already had a watertight murder case to present. Burowski was so charged, and ordered to stand trial late in September.

Feelings about the case ran high. A Parry Sound newspaper described the courtroom as crammed with "every class and condition of society from gum-chewing flappers in short skirts to care-worn mothers with crying babies." Burowski's defense revolved around the argument that the fatal bullet could as easily have come from somewhere in the surrounding darkness, fired by one of the two strangers he maintained had picked him up in the stolen car shortly before it was ditched, then left him holding the bag. In similar circumstances a court today might be satisfied with a conviction for manslaughter, but Burowski was found guilty as charged, and before the year was out was hanged in the exercise yard of the Parry Sound District Jail. As the midnight hour of execution approached, citizens thronged James Street in front of the jail, while others climbed on adjacent rooftops to glimpse the scaffold's upper framework, eerily illuminated by light from within the high-walled prison yard.

And what of the other train robber, or two others, as many people believed had to be involved in the daring scheme? The witnesses to the shooting — the Laird brothers, Claude Jackson and Roland — saw only Burowski at the ditched Buick, but to his dying day, Walter Laird would maintain that after he had Burowski pinned down, he heard additional gunshots come from somewhere else. The surrounding area was cordoned off and combed for days by police officers rushed in from all over Ontario. A dozen or more transients were picked off roads and the nearby Canadian National Railway and lodged in the Parry Sound jail, but all were eventually cleared and released.

For a long time, though, fear continued to stalk the Great North Road that someday a desperado would burst from the bush to gun down more innocent citizens.

◄○►

A three-cell lockup, stoutly built of squared logs and perched atop a steep hill behind the temperance hotel in Dunchurch, is believed to have been the only prison ever to stand along the Great North Road, aside from the substantial brick edifice in the centre of Parry Sound that, until the beginning of the 21st century, served as the district jail. Just what led to a perceived need for a jail in Dunchurch is uncertain, but it's a safe bet that the community's position as a hub of the lumbering industry, combined with the fact it boasted a liquor hotel, had much to

This is an impression of the Dunchurch jail, done by Andy Houser from descriptions left by some people who remembered it. A news item from Dunchurch dated December 1897 hints at its value as a deterrent to crime: "The jail is still on the hill, awaiting its first occupant, a little building as strong as a fort, a cold white sentinel seen from afar."

Courtesy of Andy Houser

do with it. As it happened, there was little if any need for it. Seemingly, its stout door and barred windows never once confined a law-breaker, although it is rumoured that on one occasion the village constable of the day attempted to lock up an unruly drunk who proved too big and uncooperative to manhandle up the hill. Once, though, the building was used as a pest house to isolate a logger who came out from a camp suffering from some contagious disease. Fed and cared for at arm's length through the door by community-spirited citizens, the patient survived, but later on, after the structure became derelict, there *was* a death on the premises. One summer day Barney, an old horse that had the run of the village, wandered inside to escape the flies and in so doing knocked down a prop holding the door open. After nearly 50 years, the lockup finally had a prisoner. Searchers never thought to check the old building, and old Barney died trapped inside. Around 1930 the building was disassembled, and some of the timbers were used to frame a new building elsewhere — which promptly burned down, erasing the last trace of the Dunchurch jail.

Chapter Fourteen

The Tourists Are Coming!

WHEN ASKED IN 1878 for some words on the sporting opportunities of the region for publication in *The Guide Book and Atlas of Muskoka and Parry Sound Districts,* George Kelcey of Dunchurch took pen in hand with enthusiasm. After describing the abundance of deer (he once counted 55 during a walk in a nearby winter yard), he turned to fishing:

> *The lakes abound with fish in this township. Whitestone, Shawanaga and Limestone Lake, contain pickerel, white fish, herring, suckers, catfish &c. High Lake, Upper Lake and Lorrimer Lake contain salmon [lake] trout and other fish…. The fish are easily caught. The settlers take great quantities of pickerel about the middle of May, catching them with their hands at the foot of the rapids. I went to look on one night, taking a man and a boy with me, who caught about 800 lbs of pickerel in about $1\frac{1}{2}$ hours. Quantities of herring are caught at the Narrows…in the village of Dunchurch. In Nov. '77 about 2200 lbs were caught by one man in his nets in about 14 days.*

Those "herring" were cisco, a small fish found in the deeper parts of most inland lakes. Taken in small-mesh gillnets, or in dipnets in late fall when they came to the surface to spawn, they were salted down by settlers for winter fare. Also present in some streams, but overlooked in Kelcey's report, were speckled trout, a species much coveted by the sport fishermen who were soon to come.

The *Guide Book* also trumpeted the attractions of McKellar, where

> *the traveller stretches his wearied limbs at the McKellar House, and after his carnal wants have been fully supplied by the genial host, Mr. William Thompson,…takes a bird's-eye view of the charmingly located village… The tourist will find the McKellar House a home in every sense of the word. The host, without fussy obsequiousness or fidgety and obtrusive worrying, contrives to make the guest feel perfectly at ease before he has been many hours housed in the hotel, and boats are at his command for fishing or general idling on the lakes.*

Around 1900 George Dawson began taking in deer hunters in the fall, meeting them at Dunchurch with his wagon for the 25-kilometre journey to Dawson Lake in northern Ferrie Township.

Courtesy of Dave Dawson

The writings of Duncan Macdonald provide us with the earliest accounts of sport hunting up the Great North Road. In mid-November 1873, a Mr. Wilkinson from Woodstock, Ontario, came north to Parry Sound for a hunt. He and Macdonald, together with two Indians from Parry Island, John Walker and Isaih Aissance, struck off for Dunchurch by hired rig. They found lodging first with noted woodsman John "Happy Jack" Stevenson of Fairholme, then moved on to Arthur Millin's in Dunchurch. In two weeks of hunting, the Indians managed to kill four or five deer, but Macdonald and Wilkinson, though they got some shooting, always missed. However, when they returned north at the beginning of January, Wilkinson did finally bag a doe.

Ten years later, in December 1883, Macdonald tried his luck again, this time with fellow Parry Sounder Tom Johnson as a hunting companion. "We had been figuring all fall to go up to Aumick Lake and have a little quiet still hunt…and a few days ago hitched up our nags and drove to old John Croswell's and put up for the night. A more clean and cosier home for Canadian Backwoodsmen is not be found today in the Dominion than old Uncle John's." In two days of hunting Johnson missed a running shot, but Macdonald "never saw a hair or hide." When the third day dawned unseasonably mild, "we harnessed up and made tracks for home through drenching rain."

Although they could hardly have realized it, Happy Jack Stevenson, Arthur Millin and John Croswell were dipping, however tentatively, into what would ultimately be recognized as the Great North Road's most valuable asset, its outdoor recreational potential. Gradually, the custom of taking in deer hunters from the south took hold among the settlers, and when the trickle of autumn visitors swelled to a steady flow penetrating ever deeper into the woods, hunters began appropriating abandoned lumber camp buildings as hunting camps, and still more settlers cashed in by teaming parties to and from the bush. Although the farm tractor, then the all-terrain vehicle, long ago superseded the horse as a means of getting there, the spots those hunting parties claimed as their base of operations still support deer and moose hunting camps, handed down through the generations.

———————◄○►———————

Writing to his sister in Scotland in the summer of 1892, farmer Frank Macfie of Sunny Slope remarked on the appearance of a new phenomenon, the summer tourist:

> We were at a picnic the other day of the Agricultural Society at "Ahmic Harbour"— you see we go in for nautical names here but you must remember half of the land here is water and some of our lakes are big enough to drown Scotland altogether. Our P.N. [picnic] was very enjoyable though not very well managed as some of the young people got up a baseball match between some Yankee tourists and natives and as the grounds of each were quite a piece apart it broke up the crowd and spoiled the effect. There has been quite a lot of tourists come into these pts this summer which will be a good thing if it

Moose hunting near Ahmic Harbour in 1912.

Courtesy of John Boyd/National Archives of Canada RD 48

George Dawson's vacated home on the upper Great North Road after "The Charter Lake Hunt Club" took over.

Courtesy of Dave Dawson

continues, as we can get a good market for lamb and such like. I sold mine all round for $3.00 a piece, and I only wish I had a hundred to sell.

Yes, the tourist invasion was underway, and the initial thrust came not from the direction of Parry Sound but from the east. While Parry Sound would have to wait several more years for rail access to the outside, by the mid-1880s passenger trains were running from Toronto to Burks Falls in eastern Parry Sound District, from which point steamboats provided convenient service downstream through some 25 miles of unspoiled lakes and wilderness to Ahmic Harbour. Thus the Magnetawan River system became the new sportsmen's frontier. Their tents soon gave way to permanent shelters, and by the turn of the century, the summer camp and cottage movement was firmly established on Ahmic and Wahwashkesh lakes.

George Dawson's gang of hunters clowning for the camera in their tent at Dawson's.

Courtesy of Dave Dawson

Following the Second World War, a new wave of development saw the Great North Road's bountiful legacy of smaller lakes begin to blossom with cottage subdivisions. The homesteaders' land rush of the 1870s and '80s had the effect of transferring the shorelines of most water bodies near the road from Crown to private ownership, leaving them open for later development. The rise of recreational land use dovetailed neatly with an accelerating rate of farm abandonment, easing the Great North Road community into a new era that ensured its survival. At the grassroots level, the sudden rise in value of disused acreage provided welcome windfalls for a generation that found itself with no-longer-viable farms on its hands. Summer and winter recreation, coupled with a recent trend that has seen increasing numbers of summer cottages turned into year-round homes, has now far outstripped farming and lumbering as the economic mainstay of the region.

The framework for development of this great recreation and retirement region was laid down a century earlier, when surveyor James W. Fitzgerald blazed out the route of the Great North Colonization Road.

CHAPTER FIFTEEN

James Macfie's Homestead: A Case Study

REMINISCING IN MIDDLE age, Mary Millin, whom we first met early in this book as a child of pioneers, recalled a certain feature of the Great North Road where it passed in front of her home in Dunchurch:

> The road ran over the hill instead of below where it is now. And I remember I used to climb the face of the hill instead of going around after the road was changed. In after years I chanced to be walking past the hill with a young man who had not been so long in the country. As I was looking up the hill, he said, "O'er-r the r-rough and r-rugged r-rocks the r-ragged r-rascals r-ran," and I thought to myself, "Well, how did he know that?"

Frank and Mary Macfie with the Great North Road in the background.

That young man (in fact he was 13 years older than Mary) was Frank Macfie, whom we also first encountered in the early pages. His deliberately burred comment on the local landscape and its denizens was just his way of mocking his own Scottish brogue, words with which he would continue to tease young folk right up until his death at age 94. At the beginning of the book we left Frank faced with caring for a bachelor uncle, James Macfie, who suffered a crippling injury when a tree fell on him. Any plans Frank had to resume his career as a marine engineer were put on hold, then permanently shelved when he met and, in 1883, married Mary Millin. Thus was the die cast. Frank took over James's holding beside the Great North Road and took up the life of a farmer on the Canadian frontier.

Soon after arriving, and well before his uncle's accident, Frank had put his training as a draftsman to use by drawing up plans for a new frame dwelling house and a set of log barns for storing feed and

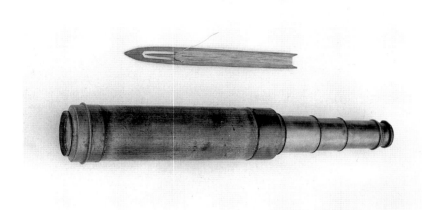

A net-maker's needle and linen twine, essential for making gillnets, and a telescope, useless on the farm, both brought by James Macfie from Scotland.

housing livestock. A year later, in the fall of 1881, he found a blank page in one of the notebooks in which he habitually jotted down or sketched things that interested him, and scribbled a summary of the past year:

Arrived here latter end of Augt. 1880 – Uncle's property & assets consisting of two lots = 240 acres 12 of which was cleared 6 felled (old chopping grown up with Briars) a log Barn small stable and a shanty. He had a cow, 2½ year old steers and one calf stock, and one plough. Crop 35 [bushels] oats 15 potatoes. I started to build a house Frame Sept. Also we put in two days logging and underbrushed ¾ acre during the fall. While building the house we lived in H. Andrews house paying 2.00 p.m. [$2 per month]. During Winter Uncle & I brought out cedar logs for a new Stable. Towards the beginning of spring we started chopping & chopped all that was underbrushed. Then we started to fell big trees in solid Bush when Uncle met with his accident (March 16) after which I could not do much work outside. On the 20th Ap. started logging & finished 24 May. Total work in [clearing?] off unburnt fallow 44 days & 12 days of a team. Changed work

Frank and Mary's daughters, Muriel, Gladys and Jessie, on the front lawn around 1915.

Courtesy of Muriel Macfie

for the help. During the summer of 81 dug out seller & embanked the house also put in most of the fence posts for a garden. Plant [undecipherable] in garden. Tried 2 successive days to get up the stable but could not manage. Hire Tom Farley. Had him 12 day @ 16 p.m. Crops turned out poor. Thrashed myself. Got 45 or 50 Bu.

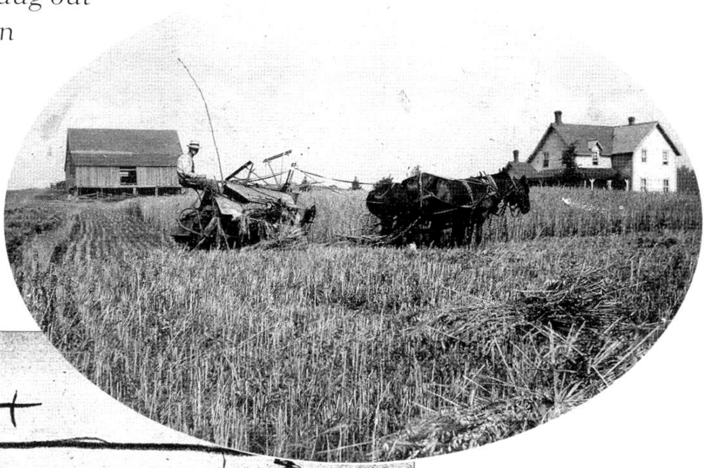

About 1901 Frank Macfie invested in a Deering grain binder, ending the tedious chore of harvesting by hand. This is his son Roy cutting oats 10 or 12 years later.

Courtesy of Muriel Macfie

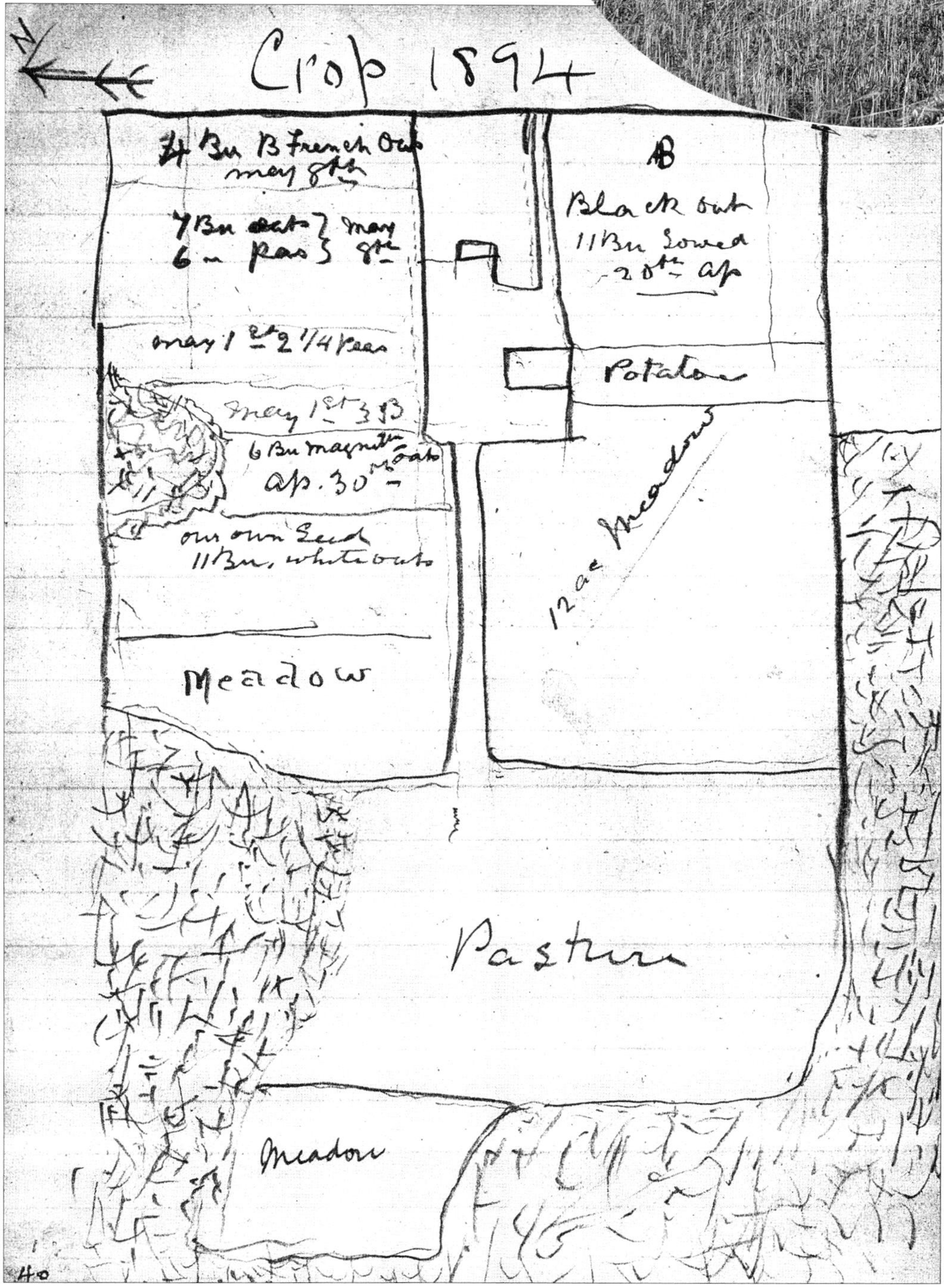

Frank Macfie kept detailed crop records. This one is from 1894.

Don Macfie, a grandson of Frank, harrowing a field in 1931, when he was ten.

Courtesy of Edith Macfie

That cedar-log barn was built to last, as have scores of identical examples that still add a rustic touch to the Ottawa Valley landscape. But only two years later, the still-unfinished building burned down, when a bonfire of chips left from the work ignited it. Then one winter day in 1895 the "dwelling house," also preserved in pencil in Frank's sketchbook, fell victim to an overheated stovepipe and went up in flames. But in each case he rebuilt bigger and better, replacing the log barns with a state-of-the-art timber-frame bank barn, reputedly the first of its kind in the vicinity, and the house with a larger and more ambitious structure than he could afford (the walls and nine-foot-high ceilings, for example, were finished in expensive tongue-and-groove hardwood). To help finance it, Frank secured a loan of one hundred pounds from a brother in the Old Country, a "blight on the family" that would not be lifted until some sons grew old enough to earn wages in the lumber woods. One distinctive feature of the old house was carried over into

Don Macfie stooking a heavy crop of oats in 1957.

the new, the concave verandah roof, an architectural accent Frank perhaps took a fancy to in his travels in the Far East.

Frank's timber-frame barn faithfully served two generations of farming Macfies and most of a third, until one September morning in 1977 when, its mows bulging with the season's crops, it was struck by lightning and reduced to ashes. The spacious home he built near the close of the 19th century, however, still shelters his descendants in the 21st.

The author of this book was raised on humorous stories about his grandfather Frank Macfie's general ineptitude as a frontier farmer, beginning with when he showed up at his first logging bee, the very air of which would be black with smoke and charcoal from the burning log piles, wearing a clean white shirt. Most of the anecdotes revolved around how, when performing some mundane chore like milking a cow or driving horses, his mind was always somewhere else, inevitably leading to a mishap of one kind or another. More at home in public life, he was instrumental in getting Hagerman Township incorporated as a municipality, and served as township clerk for its first 30 years. He sat on government commissions, took a lead in religious affairs, including the building of a fine brick Presbyterian church in Dunchurch, and was always available to sing a song or deliver a monologue at community concerts. He and Mary also sent three sons overseas in the Great War, the youngest of whom did not return.

Still, ill-suited to the farming life as he apparently (and by his own admission) was, in the 25 years following taking over from his uncle in 1880 he and Mary (their children did not begin reaching their teens until early in the new century) somehow managed to transform a tiny clearing in the woods into a farm with some

Acquiring a car was a benchmark of progress. Edith and Roy Macfie, the first four of their seven children, and their brand new 1929 Chevrolet.

Rural mail delivery continues to be a vital service on the Great North Road. Here Ritchie Macfie of Sunny Slope collects the mail in the 1950s.

Ritchie Macfie, representing the fifth generation of his family, steered the Macfie farm into the 21st century. Behind him is the home his great-grandfather built in 1896.

75 acres under cultivation. While doing so, Frank still found time to record progress in his precious notebooks, a sample of which is reproduced on page 151. The notes and diagrams give no hint of the amount of toil the couple expended in the annual round of land-clearing, cultivating, sowing, harvesting, threshing and marketing — while bearing and raising a large family — but given the rudimentary implements and facilities at their disposal, it must have been tremendous.

Frank and Mary raised seven children, the oldest of whom, Roy, assumed ownership of the farm in 1919 following his return home from four and one-half years soldiering in France and Belgium. Over the years, several hundred more forested acres had been added to James's original holding, and by conducting annual winter logging operations, starting a commercial sugarbush operation and working 16-hour days, Roy and his wife, Edith Mitchell, whom he married in 1920, kept the farm viable as they in turn raised seven children. In 1952, they handed over to their firstborn, Donald, who, together with his wife, Ilda Robertson, continued farming for 40 more years before standing aside while their oldest, Ritchie, steered the Macfie family farm, by then a beef cattle and maple syrup operation, into the 21st century.

Among the several hundred Great North Road homesteads that were taken up in the settlement years, James Macfie's stands alone as the only one to have been farmed into the fifth generation of the same family.

CHAPTER SIXTEEN

A Century Down the Road: A Portrait Gallery

"Grievious Bob" Moore's barn, framed by a dead elm and showing signs of neglect, nevertheless still stands four-square on its stone foundation.

Hops, used as a raising agent in bread-making, were grown in many gardens of the pioneers, and a few such plantings still survive as volunteers. More than a century after William Moore introduced the plant to his Sunny Slope homestead, his grandson Hector Wye respectfully permits the vines to use his woodpile as a summer climbing place.

Above: This 19th-century water-powered sawmill at Hurdville at the outlet of Manitouwabing Lake, photographed in 1955, operated into the mid-20th century.

Courtesy of Jack Thompson

Oliver Sands (left) and Dave Wye arrived in Hagerman township as children, part of a small group of migrants from Chatham, Ontario, who in the 1870s staked claims to land a kilometre or so off the Great North Road.

Above left: John "McKellar Jack" Campbell, who followed in the footsteps of his father, legendary logger Dougald, by running lumber camps and river drives himself, reminisces about a long and rewarding life.

Above: Eleanor Moore, daughter of pioneer Jim Bayne and widow of Robert "Sliver Bob" Moore.

Above: A discarded relic of a time when muscle power ruled: a farm wagon.

Right: The author interviewing Nelson Clelland of Maple Island in 1987.

Courtesy of Heather Bickle

Top: The end of the road. The Langton Carr homestead, just a few hundred metres short of where the Great North Road terminated at Commanda, survives as a monument to the hundreds of farms that once flanked the thoroughfare. The house is a fine example of the spacious frame structures replaced the log homes of the pioneers.

Middle: According to his great-grandson Dr. Ken Dickie, in his native Ireland, pioneer Thomas Dickie who homesteaded a few kilometres north of McKellar "was a penny-a-day wall builder." It followed, then, that the abundant crop of stones he found on his location would go to fence in his house and garden. Part of the wall still stands.

Bottom: A rare surviving section of the Great North Road, preserved when the road at Fairholme was rerouted around the turn of the 20th century. Here, Ky and Zena Dobson, who live nearby on land once owned by their great-grandfather Tom Bell, display ironwork from a wrecked buggy.